I'm Glad You Asked

Powerful Answers to Your Real Estate Investing Questions

Bret Ehlers

Copyright © 2016 Bret Ehlers

All rights reserved.

ISBN: 151512701X
ISBN-13: 978-1515127017

I'M GLAD YOU ASKED

DEDICATION

For weeks I struggled to find the adequate words which express my feeling of love, gratitude and describe the greatness of the three most incredible people I have known.

Marilyn is the mother of my birth. She taught me a love for life, to practice and practice the skills which increased my talents, speak publicly, and instilled the belief that I could accomplish anything. At 83 Mom is the church organist. She simultaneously plays the keys and foot pedals. She is vibrant, active and cloaked with 83 years of wisdom and foresight from her life's experiences. From the days of horse pulled wagons and outhouses to the miracles of indoor plumbing, automobiles and the technologically advanced world she sees and uses today. Mom graciously invested untold hours in spelling corrections, sentence structuring and editing the e-mail manuscripts to create readable content to help you learn. Thank You Mom.

Sylvia, my wonderful Mother-in-Law who was brave enough to introduce me to her precious daughter and the girl of my dreams. She continued to believe in me even while she watched her daughter struggle through very difficult financial times. Thank You Mom for your faith and the introduction to your wonderful daughter.

Heidi is the girl of my dreams, the love of my life and my cherished wife, companion and business partner of 35 years. In the deepest of my personal despair because of Heidi's personal strength and support I did not quit. A lesser woman would have left me in the really tough times. Even living in a $75 monthly storage shed rental after a failed business venture, Heidi still encouraged me to pursue my dreams of prosperity and personal fulfillment.

We eventually moved into our million-dollar dream home. With Heidi as my spouse and business partner I have accomplished so much more in life than I would have accomplished on my own. Thank You Heidi for loving and believing in me when the world crumbled around us.

YOUR RESPONSIBILITY TO BE ACCOUNTABLE

Your business and personal situation is one of a kind.

Business and real estate professionals may become educated by learning from each other, however you should always hire the services of industry specialists for the advice which is needed to keep your business legal, safe and to maximize your entity structuring and tax benefits.

The risk incurred by performing these specialties on your own is never worth the money you would save.

Since every state, county and city has specialized laws, the first experts you should hire would include a business and real estate tax specialist and real estate attorneys who know how to complete multi-party, simultaneous closings and seller finance transactions.

The content and sample contracts provided in this book are to give a broad knowledge of possibilities for you to earn a significant income with your own business. Only execute this information with the legal professionals you have hired to implement these strategies in helping you safely make money in your business.

The right legal and tax experts will know how to execute this information. Don't hire the others who don't have the expertise.

Table of Contents

INTRODUCTION 7

METHODOLOGY 8

CHAPTER 1 FINDING PROPERTIES 9

CHAPTER 2 MAKING OFFERS 37

CHAPTER 3 PROPERTY ANALYSIS 71

CHAPTER 4 PROPERTY REPAIRS 82

CHAPTER 5 INVESTMENT METHODS 97

CHAPTER 6 SELLING PROPERTIES 101

CHAPTER 7 YOUR BUSINESS 110

ACKNOWLEDGEMENTS 129

INTRODUCTION

Bret is my friend. I love listening to him teach people about real estate. I have an office next to him and I can hear his enthusiasm every day. One of the phrases I often hear him say is "I'm Glad You Asked". He then proceeds to answer the individual's question with clarity and passion. Bret is a great teacher and has helped an amazing number of people get started in real estate.

I've been bugging Bret for a long time to write a book. After several reminders I realized that he would never be able to do it as it would take time away from teaching the investors he loves.

So one day while he was on the phone I had the inspiration to kick him out of his chair. I then sat down and forwarded to myself a couple of weeks' worth of his emails. I then organized them into the book that you are about to read.

You will find that Bret has a great knowledge of real estate. You will also see what it is like to become a real estate investor and have your questions and concerns answered by a true Mentor and Coach. Remember - nothing is really hard in real estate investing – a new investor just needs a strong and capable guiding hand.

My hope is that you will gain confidence from reading Bret's answers and be able to move forward fearlessly as a new investor.

Mark Sanderson

METHODOLOGY

Part of the fun of this book is in seeing actual questions from real people and the actual response from Bret. No effort was made to "correct" the grammar of the questions. Somehow that would seem to take away from the authenticity of the book.

My hope is that you can feel the emotions and the concerns of the questioner and Bret's ability to provide the right answer.

I encourage the reader to see more than just Bret's answer to the question. Pay attention to how Bret builds people up and instills confidence in them. Pay attention to how Bret not only provides an answer but gives them a strategy on how to proceed. Bret loves to give people the tools that they need to succeed.

Bret is constantly updating his information and materials. Be sure to visit him on LinkedIn: www.linkedin.com/in/bret-ehlers-149b3311

Mark Sanderson

CHAPTER 1 FINDING PROPERTIES

I'M GLAD YOU ASKED

Hi Bret,

Wishing You & your Wife a Happy 35th Anniversary today!!

On the call tonight, when you were on the subject of the Real Estate agents. Could you send some examples of the questions you ask them?

They were some Great question.

Thanks so much!

Here is the script I use to perform a job interview for buyer's agents.

IMPORTANT: YOU MAY NOT NEED TO ASK ALL OF THE QUESTIONS BELOW IF THE AGENT HAS SHARED THE INFORMATION WITH YOU OR IT IS IN THE MLS ADS.

a. (YOU) Hi, I'm calling about the home for sale at <property address>.
   (AGENT) (Yes) how can I help you?

b. (YOU) Are you the listing agent?
   (Agent) Yes

c. (YOU) Wonderful. Have you been in the property?
   (Agent) Yes

d. (YOU) Great! Is there anything else that you can tell me about the house that is not in the MLS ad? (Let them ramble about the property...) Complete the "Property Information Worksheet" as they talk.

e. (YOU) What upgrades have been done to the property since it was built.

f. (YOU) Perfect, that sounds like exactly what I am looking for. Tell me, on a scale of 1 to 10, with 10 being the best, how would you rate the current condition of the home? (It's a 7) Okay a 7, what would make it a 10? (Let them answer and take notes)

g. (YOU) Okay, does the property need anything else or have any deferred maintenance that I would need to repair? (Let them answer)

h. (YOU) Excellent! If all that work was done and this home was a "10", what would that list price look like compared to what the home is listed for now? (Let them give you the ARV)

i. (YOU) How much money do you think I would have to put into the home to make it a 10? (Let them give you a dollar amount)

j. (YOU) Did you receive the repair costs from a contractor?

k. (YOU) Wonderful! Can you tell me if the Seller is highly motivated or are they just testing the market? (Try to determine the Sellers motivation and timing)

l. (YOU) Thanks for sharing that with me. Just out of curiosity, is the seller open and receptive to Seller Financing for a short period of time?

m. If "No", (YOU say): Okay, no problem.

n. If "Yes", (YOU say): Fantastic! Do you know what type of terms they would consider? (Write down their answer)

o. (YOU) Now, how should my real estate agent go about scheduling a showing for me or submitting an offer if I'm interested? (Write down their answer)

OBJECTION HANDLERS:

1. Are you looking for a home for yourself or someone else?
   YOUR ANSWER: I'm looking for a great deal for myself.

2. Are you working with a Buyer's Agent?
   YOU ANSWER: Yes, but they are not available at the moment and I saw this home online and was so excited about it that I just had to call right away.

3. Are you pre-qualified for a home loan?
   YOUR ANSWER: Yes, my agent has my pre-approval letter.

4. Are you a real estate investor?
   YOUR ANSWER: I am a home buyer looking for a good deal and I would prefer to buy a home that I can fix up for some immediate equity.

5. Have you called me before with these same questions on another property?
   YOUR ANSWER: I may have. I have been in the market for a home for quite some time and I am still looking for a really

good deal and I would prefer to buy a home that I can fix up for some immediate equity.

It's a terrific day!

Coach Bret Ehlers

Hi Bret, We Thank you for the Great information! We were wanting you to look at the attached property information we found on Zillow. Since this does say Auction & the property is in Foreclosure. Our question is, since Zillow says From $44,000. Would this type of property be something to look into further or would it be too risky since it is in auction?

We are looking at FSBO's, Foreclosures, & Pre-Foreclosures.

We Thank You for your time!

Good Morning,

Inasmuch as I do not have a completed "Property Worksheet" from the real estate agent interview I am unable to give a determination on the property.

A few notes about auctions.

We have many students that participate in various auctions. These venues can be an exceptional place to buy a profitable property. Because of technology, participating in online auctions is easier than ever before to purchase real estate anywhere in the world. This has added additional competition pressure for winning an auction property at the correct formula price.

You must also be very careful of fraudulent activities on these auction sites. We recently learned of someone who was the successful bidder for a property that was auctioned on Ebay. The individual sent the money directly to the Ebay seller via Western Union. I wish they had used Pay Pal instead. When the student went to the property it was a vacant lot. His bid was for a house on that lot.

The seller had marketed and presented a house with a lot on the Ebay auction site. The seller refused to refund the money and Ebay informed the individual that they do not guarantee Ebay real estate auctions; only auctions for trinkets.

Now, they found that there are title issues for just the ownership of the lot. What looked to be a great deal has become a nightmare for this person.

There are some precautions I want to share with you:

1. Auctions are set up to invoke human emotion: Fear of loss and greed.
2. Be aware of the hidden auction fees. Carefully study their website so you are proficient with the rules of THEIR game.
3. Unless it is a Government auction, always place your money with your Title Company or closing attorney.
4. Make sure you always receive a Warranty Deed or General Warranty Deed with title insurance in exchange for your hard earned money on all real estate transactions.
5. Never accept a Special Warranty Deed or Quit Claim Deed for any real estate deed transfer. Especially be aware of this trick to cheat you on properties that are being sold by banks for their distressed REO's and foreclosed government properties.
6. I would also call and interview the listing agent where the property has representation.
7. Calculate the formula from the information on your "Property Info Worksheet". That never changes.
8. Do not bid above the Maximum Offer Formula you calculated before the auction began.

Safe investing in real estate is the key to profitability.
Talk Soon.

Coach Bret Ehlers

PROPERTY INFO WORKSHEET
(What you need to know about the seller and the property)

DATE OF CONTACT: _____

I'M GLAD YOU ASKED

List Price: _____ ARV: _____ Rental Y___N__

Seller Finance Yes: ____ No: ____ Terms:
_____
_____

_____

List Agents / Owner Name: _____

Phone Number: _____

E-Mail: _____

Property Address / Zip Code:
_____

Year Built: _____

Square Footage of Building: _____
Beds:_____ Baths:_____

Property Condition 1-10: _____
Cost of Repairs: _____

Building   Upgrades
_____
_____
_____

Dates: Roof_____ HVAC_____ Electrical_____ Plumbing_____
Windows_____ Pool_____

Repairs Needed:
_____
_____

_____
_____
_____

Seller Motivation:
_____
_____

NOTES:
_____
_____
_____
_____
_____

Instructions for Property Access:
_____

Certified Bank Appraisal: _____

Days on the market: _____

How much is left owing on the home: _____

Bret,

I recently got a rehab investor call me as he is unable to sell his house. He has done work on the house and listed it on the MLS at $299K and it has been there for over 30 days. ARV: $325K

He disclosed to me that the house needs to be connected to the city sewer system and that a small bridge needs to be constructed which costs around $30K. He has the necessary permits for each job from the city.

He is looking for Cash buyers to take over this house from him as low as $175K. But he is not willing to put the house under contract or contingencies with me to wholesale the deal. He says if I bring him a cash buyer he is willing to show the property and give him the lock box code so that they can do their due diligence.

How do I go about advertising this property to my cash buyers if I don't have a contract for this house? If my buyers are interested in this property, how do I go about getting the transaction done?

Your help is much appreciated.

Good Morning Stan,

It is always great to hear from you.

In answer to your question on marketing:

You do not market any properties where you do not have a contract with the seller. In order to stay legal as a wholesaler you must place the property under contract with the owner.

This can be a Non-Exclusive Option or Standard Purchase and Sales

Agreement with an extended closing date to market the property.

The real estate agents in your market are going out of their way to find investors without property contracts so they can turn you into the State.

Without a contract with the seller you will be accused of representing real estate without a real estate license and the state will levy very expensive fines and penalties.

This has occurred with two new investors I have worked with who felt uncomfortable getting the contract from the seller. They were turned in to the State by a real estate agent as the new investor marketed the property. I guarantee, dealing with the State was far more uncomfortable than getting the contract from the seller.

If the seller is unwilling to enter into a real estate contract with you, I recommend you pass on that property and find other properties.

HERE ARE THE STEPS TO COMPLETING A WHOLESALE TRANSACTION:

1. Place the property under contract with the seller using a Non Exclusive Option of Purchase and Sales Agreement.
2. Contact all of your investors with cash whom you have interviewed, who can close on the property in two or three days.
3. For your extra protection, have these cash investors sign a Non-Circumvention Agreement before you take them to the property.
4. To save your time and only work with the serious investors, schedule all of the investors to arrive at the same time at the property.

5. Let the investors know that whoever gives you the most money and can close in two or three days, with cash, will buy the property.
6. Enter into a Purchase and Sales contract with the successful investor.
7. Meet the property owner and the investor with cash at the Title Company or closing attorney, for a simultaneous closing.
8. Deposit the payday check you received at the closing in your bank.

HERE IS SOME INFORMATION ON THE USE OF THE NON-EXCLUSIVE OPTION CONTRACT. THIS IS MY FAVORITE FOR WHOLESALING:

1. The Non-Exclusive Option (NEO) gives you the right to control the property and sell the contract without the obligation to purchase the property.
2. The NEO gives the seller the right to continue to market the property and even hire a real estate agent. No matter what the owner does with his/her own marketing you have the "First Right of Refusal".
3. NOTE: The seller generally feels a huge relief after entering into the agreement with you and they stop marketing the property.
4. We negotiate a predetermined price with the seller for the lowest possible price on the property as part of the NEO. We also set the terms of the agreement and establish that the seller will continue to pay all of the monthly payments until the closing, including the transaction closing costs.
5. All "Contract Terms" of the NEO are negotiable. We want all the terms in our favor. The seller wants all the terms in his/her favor. We agree somewhere in the middle.

6. You are paid the difference between the contract price with the seller in the NEO and the sales price paid by your buyer.
7. You pay no closing costs whenever possible.
8. The Non-Exclusive Option works great for wholesaling retail properties also.

Yahooooo! There is no liability or financing required with the seller to do these transactions. In order for another investor to be interested in purchasing a wholesale property from you, be sure to place the property under contract at the correct price.

NOTE: Every seller wants more than the property is worth. You will learn how to negotiate the price down.

1. The foundation numbers to calculate all offers is the AFTER REPAIR VALUE (ARV). This is the price the property will sell in 30 days after the repairs are completed. You bet your financial life on this figure. Can the property really be sold for the determined ARV in 30 days? Your financial life is depending on this number.

2. Even when you are not doing the repairs you must know the close repairs costs to accurately place the property under contract in order to wholesale the property to another investor with cash. For our example let's use $100,000 ARV.

3. Profit for your bank account: 20% of the ARV is subtracted from the ARV for your profit.

4. Expenses for your transaction: 10% of the ARV is subtracted from the ARV. This is the expense for closing costs to acquire and resell the property, property tax while you possess the property, insurance, utilities, etc.

5. Costs for the renovation of the real estate: This should be bid to at least 2 or more contractors. Be sure to itemize, in writing, every nail that you want repaired on the property so you get an accurate, competitive bid price from the contractors.

HERE ARE THE NUMBERS:

$100,000 ARV

$20,000 PROFIT SUBTRACTED FROM THE ARV = $80,000

$10,000 EXPENSES SUBTRACTED FROM THE ARV = $70,000

$40,000 CONSTRUCTION EXPENSES SUBTRACTED FROM THE ARV = $30,000

$5,000 WHOLESALING FEE SUBTRACTED FROM THE ARV = $25,000

$25,000 IS YOUR MAXIMUM OFFER TO SUBMIT.

IF THE SELLER DOES NOT ACCEPT THE ACCURATE OFFER WE GO TO THE NEXT PROPERTY.

YOU WANT TO MAKE MONEY WITH THE PROPERTY WHEN YOU PURCHASE IT.

Now you can go make some serious income!

I will look forward to helping you with your transactions.

It is a terrific day!

Bret Ehlers

Bret, I know we have not been the A pupil students but we ran up against two jobs that came in back to back and are running us a little ragged. But I did make time to go to my City hall and asked if they had some distressed properties. They gave me this home page from an excel sheet with a list as follows. My question for you is, I would like to make up a letter to the owners and the banks that are on this list, but I want to use the right wording and sound professional without throwing it in the round file. Could you please advise?

It is good to hear from you.

Jobs come first. It is the income from your job that allows you to build a successful real estate investing business.

Below are some tips for making contact with the owner occupants:

The owner who lost the house to the Trustee or Sherriff's sale has a foreclosed property.

Banks do not have foreclosed properties.

Banks have:

1. Bank Owned Properties
2. Real Estate Owned (REO) Properties
3. Non-Performing Assets

All three terms mean the same thing. Through legal process the bank has sold at auction or taken the real estate that collateralized the defaulted loan of the seller.

You will not be able to access the properties owned by large banks unless you are buying a package of a couple hundred properties.

Most of these REO properties are listed with national real estate brokers who have contracted a commission discount to represent the lender. Unless you have millions to purchase an REO package you will not be buying the property directly from the bank unless it is a small local bank or credit union.

With vacant properties which are not bank owned, properties in probate or pre-foreclosure actions, you must contact the executor or owner of the property. The owner is in full control of the property until the final gavel falls at the auction. Do not waste your time calling the Financial Institution, Trustee, Sherriff or the courts. They are unable to help you. You must work with the owner or their appointed representative such as an attorney or real estate broker.

All properties you encounter will have the property owner information at the County Recorder's Office. This is also where Public Notices are posted prior to public advertising in the newspapers and online.

Most State Statutes require the default and sales notices to be advertised in your local newspaper under the Legal Notices section. Some counties will also advertise online in addition to the newspaper.

For Tax Lien and Deed Auctions the information will be posted at the County Treasurer's Office, newspapers, online and at the Recorder's office.

This is all you need to know. Start contacting the sellers with default notices.

This is important: Everything I do is to be effective and different from the real estate agents and other investors in the market. You want to stand out in the crowd!

1. TARGET MARKETS – Where To Find Defaulted Properties:
   a. DO NOT BUY LISTS UNTIL YOU TALK WITH THE COACHING TEAM FIRST
   b. Most lists are not what they are represented to be
   c. Notice of Default (NOD)
   d. Notice of Trustee or Sheriff's Sale
   e. Death Certificates
   f. Business Owners
   g. Assisted Living Establishments
   h. Military Organizations such as Veterans of Foreign Wars
   i. Divorce Filings
   j. Bankruptcy Filings
   k. And many more categories (ask for the 60+ ways to find a property)
2. FINDING THE PHONE NUMBER OF THE OWNER/SELLER:
   a. Do this search from the comfort of your home
   b. Search on the internet the name of the owner and the property address
   c. Google, Bing, etc.
   d. Facebook
   e. Linkedin
   f. www.411.com
   g. www.whitepages.com
   h. Neighbors
3. LETTER MESSAGE:

   My wife and I, or, I am looking to purchase a home in your neighborhood without a Real Estate Agent. If your home or another home in the neighborhood is for sale without a real estate agent please give Heidi and me a call. Xxx-xxx-xxxx

It is a terrific day!

Bret and Heidi Ehlers

4. CONSTRUTION OF THE LETTER:
   a. When sending a letter to a vacant property, write the following on the front of the envelope: "Forwarding Service Requested". Your letter will be forwarded to the new address and the Post Office will send you a card with the new forwarded address information.
   b. NOTE: Your name and return address must be on the envelope if you expect to receive the forwarding information from the Post Office on the vacant property.
   c. Use an invitation size envelope in yellow or pink.
   d. Hand writing the send and return address on the envelope is a must.
   e. Have the message written on a card that is not folded in the envelope. When it is pulled from the envelope it takes no effort to read.
   f. Do not have a business name anywhere on the communication.
   g. When time permits, it is best to hand write the content inside the envelope, as well.
   h. Hand sign the card in the envelope. Again, no business card!
   i. A spritz of perfume. We are wanting to be different.
   j. I have already stated that I want to buy a home in the letter. That is all that I need to say.
5. WHEN AT THE DOOR FOR A LIVE ENCOUNTER:
   a. I never present the defaulted owner a business card.

b. Have the person at the door get a pen and paper to write down YOUR name and phone number in their hand writing.
  c. At the door my approach is the same as the letter. I am looking to buy a home in the neighborhood, without a real estate agent…..
6. DOES BULK MAILING WORK:
  a. Standard rate of return is less than half a percent. If you send out one thousand letters you will receive approximately five responses. Some areas may yield a higher conversion rate.
  b. The reason for the low rate of return is the home owner does not trust us or any other person sending them a letter to buy their house.
  c. That is why I recommend that you contact everyone who knows who you are and let them know you are buying real estate, and, helping people with difficult real estate problems. They already trust you.

Ask for additional information for helping you to work with the seller and not offend them with your initial contact.

There are several possibilities for innovative solutions to help the home owner.

Yes, for cash we do need to pay approximately 50% less than the property could be sold in 30 days after the repairs are completed.

You never let the seller stay in the house or let them move back in after the transaction is complete.

Here are some other solution possibilities:

1. Forbearance with the bank and place the back payments to the back of the loan and you take over the payments.
2. Short Sale and either wholesale the property or fix and flip it.
3. After the seller moves out, bring the payments current and have a tenant make the payments on the seller's mortgage
4. Fund and close an outright purchase if there is enough equity in the property.
5. A loan modification, and after the seller moves out, make the payments on the loan.
6. BENEFITS TO THE SELLER:
    a. Stops the harassment from the bank, legal letters, investors contacting them to buy their home and the embarrassment that goes with the public notices for the auction
    b. Eliminate a foreclosure from being placed on their credit report
    c. Keep their credit score from dropping further
    d. Eliminate a deficiency judgment
    e. Eliminate income tax penalties from deficiency of the originated loan
    f. Help from possible loss of employment
    g. Help from possible reduction in wages, if government employee
    h. Help from increases in their auto insurance premium
    i. Help from increases in their property and casualty insurance premium
    j. Help from additional increases in their credit card interest rate
    k. Helps them to be able to rent a new place to live

    l. If there is equity, they may receive some equity in the sale to you
    m. The house is no longer holding them back from moving on with their life

Payment defaults and vacant properties are another avenue to purchase properties for a successful transaction.

To Your Success

It is a terrific day!

Coach Bret Ehlers

I am looking at a property that is listed on two different sites & two different dollar amounts. It is close to about a $50,000 difference. One site is an auction site. I have tried calling the listed realtor, but have only been able to talk to an operator so far. Hmmm....

So how can they list the property this way? Has anyone else ran into this?

The official real estate agent advertising site is the local board Multiple Listing Service where the property is located. The MLS ad will be posted by the licensed real estate agent who has paid dues to post their listed property on the local board Multiple Listing Service (MLS).

All listing information on this site must be accurate and include full disclosures of information known to the listing agent. There are laws in each State which govern the Multiple Listing Service and property postings. For the most accurate information, you will want to view the property ad postings on the local Multiple Listing Service where the property is located.

The National Association of Realtors (NAR) is an attempt to unite the licensed real estate agents throughout the United States. A REALTOR designation is purchased by a licensed real estate agent when annual dues are paid to the National Association of Realtors. It is like a union. The NAR is a special interest group which lobbies in Washington on behalf of real estate agents and provides other services to represent real estate agents in the United States.

The NAR ties into most local MLS systems using the website www.realtor.com Information on this site is as accurate as the posted information on the local Multiple Listing Service which is governed by each state. Posting on this site may be delayed in uploading from the local MLS systems.

All other real estate websites such as Zillow, Redfin, Trulia, etc. are privately held ventures which attempt to expose properties for sale to the public and do not have to abide by any standard. Do not use these sites for comps. The information has been found to be inaccurate more that 50% of the time.

Auction sites such as HUBZU deliberately price a property at "too good to be true" prices to suck you in to bid in their auctions. Be very careful of hidden fees. You may have to pay the real estate listing commission should you be the successful bidder buyer.

To Your Success

It is a terrific day!

Coach Bret Ehlers

I have been on Realtor.com and filling out property info worksheets, however, never seem to get all the info needed to start negotiation. Am I the only one? I need some serious tips.

For Sale By Owner, real estate agent and buyer interviews are the same as learning script lines for a play.

You have a script to memorize and perform. If you miss your lines the dialogue of the play falls apart and the audience is lost.

When I performed in plays I practiced for hours and hours memorizing my lines and executing the scenes with the other participants in the production.

In real estate I have invested thousands of hours practicing my scripts so I executed well my communication and receive the results I wanted to achieve. I was uncomfortable at first, just like all new investors.

I love to watch the growth and success of new investors who learn their scripts and have success.

When I learned to override my gut default and executed my script, I achieved the results I wanted.

The more I practiced 'perfect practice' the better I became. You can too!

To Your Success

It is a terrific day!

Coach Bret Ehlers

What would I do at an Investor's club?

You can make great contacts and find properties! Here are some tips to make your local investor club a transaction source:

1. You are new to investing so don't pretend otherwise. It is OK for you to say "I am just getting started".

   Spend 90% of your time asking questions about how they do real estate investing and listen.

2. There is no need to tell them you are in a real estate coaching program. You are at the club meeting to find out what properties the members may have available to you for a profitable transaction.

3. The only real investors in the club are the investors that present properties and opportunities in front of the group at each club meeting.

   You want to introduce yourself and get connected to those investors. Ask what you could do to participate in bringing transactions to them?

4. The rest of the members at the club meeting are there for the association, beer and pretzels.

   Be careful not to get sucked into the big talkers that have no transaction to present to the club each week.

   They have a big story but no transaction or investment property ownership.

   I know a fellow that has not done a transaction in years and owns no investment real estate.

   To hear him talk you would think he owns all of Phoenix. In Texas they call this the "Big Hat, no Cattle" syndrome.

Ask how many property transactions they have completed in the last 180 days and how many properties they own.

Be sure you join the ranks of the first group with properties!

To Your Success

It is a terrific day!

Coach Bret Ehlers

How does an assumable mortgage work? Do you have to assume the entire amount of the mortgage? Is it negotiable?

Seller financing is alive and well where we make the payments for the seller on their loan.

All assumable mortgages are gone.

After the failure of the Savings and Loan industry in the 80's, assumable mortgages were phased out.

You may come across a VA or FHA loan that has a "Qualifying Assumption" clause.

These loans can be assumed for about $650.00. The new borrower must qualify for these loans in the same manner as initiating a new loan. You need to know that there is a "Recourse Clause". Should the assuming buyer default on the loan the responsibility for the loan converts to the original borrower.

Thank you for your response. We did a search and found about 160 homes in the Atlanta market for sale that are marked as Assumable mortgages. Do you think that is accurate? Do you think they are really "seller financing"? I realize that seller financing is the better deal for us.

I commend you for finding the properties to work with.

These properties could be FHA / VA qualifying assumable loans. There are not many of those loan products available these days.

Yes they could be seller finance properties as well.

Real estate is a wonderful treasure hunt.

I encourage you to give the seller a call and find out what they are selling.

The best outcome will allow you to acquire a profitable property.

The second best event is an addition of more sellers, real estate agents or investors with cash to your contact data base.

Let me know what you find.

To Your Success

It is a terrific day!

Coach Bret Ehlers

CHAPTER 2 MAKING OFFERS

Bret, Can you pass along your information you have regarding earnest money and why we only give 100 dollars?

Good Morning,

All you need to consummate a real estate transaction in many governing jurisdictions is the promise of the buyer to purchase the property and the promise of the seller to sell the property to that buyer.

When actual consideration is required, $10 or less in cash, merchandise, an exchange of service or Love and Affection is all that is needed to satisfy contract law for Earnest Money.

I encourage you to risk no more than $100 earnest money with your offers. As active investors you will be placing several offers each week. With $100 earnest money placed with each offer you could have earnest money commitments of $2,000 to $3,000 each month.

When the Seller preforms and accepts your offer all remaining funds for your transaction will be provided by you to your Title Company or Closing Attorney to open escrow and close.

Real estate agents will tell you that you must place a $1000 or more in earnest money with your offer. When you informed them you will only place $100 in earnest money they will say $100 earnest money makes your offer look weak.

Earnest money fulfills contract law. It does not show the strength of the commitment to purchase the property.

Earnest money for bank owned or HUD properties will generally need to be more than $100. You need to decide if you are willing to risk more than $100 with your offer.

The Banks and Government have added their own attorney created contract as an addendum to your State required real estate agent contract. This action negates the equal protection provided to the buyer and the seller in the state contract. The one sided bank and government contract addendum is against you. The bank and government contact requires you to perform as per the bank or HUD if you want to place an offer. The contract is in favor of the bank and the government, not you.

Let me introduce you to the politics of earnest money. The real estate agents may break the law by not presenting your offer to the seller if you do not place $1000 or more in earnest money with your offer. Do you have $1,000.00 ready for earnest money? Are you able to handle the loss of $1000.00?

A few weeks ago a student in Florida placed an offer on a bank owned property in Florida. She chose to discard our instruction and placed her last $3500 as earnest money with her offer.

Her offer was accepted and within the inspection period contingency she found more building damage than was originally expected. She rescinded her offer and placed demand for return of the earnest money since she had performed within the terms of her accepted offer.

The bank told her she would have to sue them to get the earnest money back. We have had similar situations with students on government owned properties.

Just because you have an accepted contract offer does not mean the seller will honor it. Your earnest money will always be at risk. At $400 per hour you will eat up your earnest money fast when you have an attorney sue to have the money returned.

In fairness to the Real Estate Agent and the Seller, does the property offer meet the buying formula? Are you truly prepared and committed to following through and purchase the property? We don't want to waste the time of the real estate agent or seller.

OFFER PRECAUTIONS TO PROTECT YOUR EARNEST MONEY

1.   Earnest money requirements above $100 are demands set by the real estate agents not by the laws.

2.   When placing your offer, submit a photo copy of your earnest money check with your offer and black out the bank routing and checking account numbers on the copy. A photo copy of a check is just as valid to cash as the original check instrument.

3.   In your offer contract you will provide the actual earnest money funds when the seller performs and accepts your offer.

4.   Hard money loans are not cash. Make your hard money offer contingent on financing if you are unable to have real cash in a couple of days.

5.   The most you want to place at risk for earnest money is $100.00.

6.   Should the listing agent and seller want to see more money in the offer, place additional non-earnest money funds at your title company to open escrow.

7.   Have your property inspection contingency for at least 14 business days.

8.   Best of all find the property ahead of the real estate agents and earnest money generally is never an issue.

Do not allow the real estate agents to extort or push you around concerning the earnest money. It is your money that pays their commission and purchases the property. You are the customer.

It's a terrific day!

Hi Bret. We have a question for you on this house that we have been going round and round about for months now.

Our offer was we were going to take over their home equity loan up to $75k and make the payments for them for six months. However, they really owe $79k and now the seller wants us to pay $800 a month when his payments are only $250. We think this is to make up for the almost $5k difference in the actual loan amount they owe.

A couple questions:

1. When you devised this offer for us were you anticipating that we would be paying the taxes monthly for them or were you thinking we should pay the taxes at closing?

2. We haven't even got to the insurance issue but our agent seems to think they are adding in the cost of the insurance.

We would like to finalize this if it is something we can move forward with.

Good Morning,

At the end of the day are you going to make money? Your negotiations would be based on that premise.

So, you are the only buyer interested in this house.
That gives you the leverage. They owe more than the house is worth with the needed repairs. What is the reasoning behind the $800.00? If the payment is $250 and the house is under water, the rest of the money needs to go to repairs.

I figured the taxes and insurance were in the monthly payment escrow of $250 a month. Are they?

If the payment does not include the taxes and insurance and paying the $800 a month IS for taxes and insurance, I would have those funds managed by a third party escrow company and not given to the seller. Who knows what they would do with the money.

Mortgage payments are paid in arears. That means July's payment pays for June's occupancy. If you are taking possession August 1st your first payment would not be due until September 1st. The taxes and insurance may be for the actual month.

Please let me know the rest of the story so I can give proper direction for this transaction.

It is a terrific day!
Coach Bret Ehlers

What is an extended closing?

When you need to reduce your expenses to rehab the property in order to increase the amount of the offer to the seller and keep your profit. We can do this with an extended 180 day closing.

There are no correct or incorrect terms for this transaction. The contract will need to meet the needs of the property, the seller and you. Having a listing agent in the middle of a seller involved transaction can make it more difficult.

The agent is afraid of protecting his/her commission.
Very few real estate agents understand the process of legally protecting the seller and their property.

When anyone is uneducated or afraid, they say "no".

In my approach with the listing agent the first thing I want to know: Is the motivation driving the sale?

Secondly, will the seller participate in seller financing?

This interview is in the "New Listing Agent Script".

Ask what the seller needs to accomplish FIRST before you say anything about what you are going to do.

Here are some bullet points we could discuss with the agent for purchasing the property:

1. The Buyer will purchase the property and close at the Title Company with the seller. (Closing Attorney).
2. The Buyer will have three days to inspect the property after signed acceptance of the offer by the seller.
3. The Buyer will purchase the property, as is.
4. The Buyer will make monthly payments to the seller's escrow company for this agreement.

5. The existing financing will remain in place on the property up to 180 days and the closing date.
6. The Seller's escrow company will send payments directly to the mortgage company, for principle, interest, taxes and insurance.
7. The Buyer will be given immediate possession of the property upon signed acceptance of this offer. The transaction time-line will begin once the buyer is given access to the property.
8. As a favor to the seller, the buyer will dispose of unwanted items and trash after the seller has taken all desired items.
9. The buyer will be responsible for the maintenance and repairs on the property during this agreement.
10. The Buyer will perform the needed repairs to prepare the property for the buyer's loan inspection and funding.
11. The buyer may assign this agreement.
12. The purchase price of the property will be the remaining balance of the unpaid mortgage which shall not exceed $75,000.00. The loan balance will be verified prior to the Buyer accepting the terms of the agreement.
13. The seller will be responsible for the listing contract.
14. Buyer and Seller will pay typical split closing costs.
15. The closing date will be before or on the last business day of the following month of the 180 days after the offer is accepted by the seller.
16. This agreement would be officially executed by the real estate attorney at the Title Company to include all protections and provisions of our mutual agreement.

There are many more possibilities depending on the needs of the seller. It is not a sure thing but an alternative offer to present.

Hope that helps you.

It's a terrific day!

Coach Bret Ehlers

I'M GLAD YOU ASKED

Bret,

I am going to try to call you tonight but if I don't get a hold of you here is my questions:

This same realtor you said I should not sign the attached contract with because you said "I would not sign it because of the clause that says if they bring you a property and you don't buy it you still have to pay a commission."

He won't put our offer in until we sign the buyer's paperwork. What would you change on the contract to make it ok for us to sign? He needs something.

These are very good questions.

Real Estate Agents are notorious for expecting you to commit to a performance guarantee for their commission with no performance guarantee from the real estate agent or broker to the financial success of your transaction or a commitment to bring you a profitable property while your hands are tied in their contract.

THEIR contract gives them the advantage. The contract is referred to as the Broker / Buyer Representation Contract or Buyer / Broker Agreement. If you have entered into this contract as an investor it really stinks for you.

I do not believe you should reward a non performing real estate broker or agent. No work has been done by an agent who sends a ticker tape of properties to your e-mail from an electronically set filter from the MLS system with no verifying comps. The agent should not expect you to pay a commission on those properties. You can find all of those properties on the MLS without an agent. Only when the agent prescreens the properties and provides comps on those properties has the agent begun to earn his/her commission.

I do believe in protecting the commission of a performing agent who has brought you a property with the verifying comps. They deserve to be paid.

Here are the parameters for signing a "Buyer / Broker Agreement".

    1. It is only for the property which they brought to you with comps to prove the value.
    2. When they are fighting for your offer to be accepted on a property.
    3. No all-inclusive agreements of services except for each property offer.
    4. There is no guarantee to pay them a commission should the transaction blow up and fall apart.
    5. After the one transaction is funded and complete, you have no further obligation to the real estate broker / agent until the next transaction offer.

Concerning the agent's remark: "I won't place your offer until you sign the agreement".

1. You can amend all contracts to be more fair and in your favor.
2. Fine. Go place the offer through one of your other 12 buyers' agents that appreciate your business and understand that you are the customer and should be treated well.
3. Pass on the deal.

I prefer the other two options. LOL

Coach Bret Ehlers

I'M GLAD YOU ASKED

Hi Bret,

I have a friend student that I'm trying to help.

He has a property under contract that he did a cash offer on (planning on using hard money) and the seller's attorney doesn't like the clause "subject to appraisal for lender" obviously because it's supposed to be a cash deal. They had that in there as one of their escape clauses.

What advice would you give on a situation like that?

Thanks for your help!

This was an investor error. Could be costly and lose the offer.

The contingency should have read:

"Subject to the property appraising for the offer price".

They should not have mentioned any lender even though a lender may be involved.

Hope that helps you.

It's a terrific day!

Coach Bret Ehlers

Coach Bret,

Here is a property from the same agent as before. Can you please review the documents we are required to sign before we sign anything? We do not feel comfortable signing anything without someone's expert knowledge.

Good Morning

You are to the point in your business where you should have professionals you work with on your team in your business.

I recommend you have a Title Company with a real estate attorney on staff. (Interview Below)

The title company attorneys have given Heidi and me a great deal of contract review as part of the closing.

The question I ask the attorney: What is in this contact that will hurt me?

At the end of the day that is the real question with the contracts.

Talk Soon.

It's a terrific day!

Coach Bret Ehlers

TITLE COMPANY or CLOSING ATTORNEY NEEDED

A Title Company is one of your key team members. The Title Company interview is completed over the telephone. There is no need to see them until you have a property to purchase or sell.

The services of a Title Company or closing attorney is needed for the research to be sure that there are no liens on the property, the chain of title and recording the transfer of the property to the new owner at the county recorder's office. The Title Company is also the protective barrier you need for all transactions where you exchange funds for real estate, especially when you pay for hard money points and fees to receive hard money funds.

There are scams where people will tell you they have the hard or private money you need and all you need to do is send the point funds, Western Union, and they will send you their funds. DO NOT DO THIS. Only exchange your funds through your Title Company or closing attorney. The following is an interview for finding a qualifying Title Company or closing attorney. I prefer to have a real estate attorney on staff at the Title Companies that I use. Many times you will get legal advice at no charge as part of the closing.

INTERVIEWING FOR A QUALIFYING TITLE COMPANY OR CLOSING ATTORNEY:

Hi, my name is _____

I buy real estate and I am looking for a Title Company where I can close my transactions.

I need to know if your company provides the services that I need.

1. First of all, do you have a full time real estate attorney on staff? Need a yes.

2. Second, do you perform multi-party and simultaneous closings? (You can also refer to this as a Concurrent Closing) You need a yes. (A simultaneous or concurrent closing is when there are more than two individuals closing on a transaction such as when you wholesale the property to another investor. You do not want to be on title at the closing. You want the title to pass around you and record to the end buyer).

3. Now this is not a deal breaker but does your company provide monthly escrow services for monthly rents and bill pay? Yes is good.

It looks as though you have the services I need.

Do you have a pen and paper handy? Again my name is _____

Which e-mail should I use to send you my contact information?

I will be sending this information for... (Your e-mail address)

I will also need you to attach your fee schedule and send it back to me. When can I expect to receive your information?

I will contact you concerning my next closing.

Thank you for your help.

(Your Name)

Bret,

Hopefully you've gotten a chance to review the corrections I've made on the offer contract. I sent the same revisions to the listing agent who is also our buyer's agent for this property, and he said that there were some problems with our contract. His response is below.

Just to give you a little back ground about this Realtor; He used to be a real estate attorney, and a rehabber. When we interviewed him, he said that he is a part of the International President's Elite here in California.

The questions we have are:

1. How would you respond to his reply if you chose him as your buyer's agent?

2. Would you be willing to speak with him?

"The attorneys for the sellers of the property are not likely to allow the listing to remain under any buyer's control for as long as 60 days with only a $500.00 deposit. Further, I am sure that a credit card payment of the deposit is not acceptable either by the seller or by the escrow company. Even further, if you want to nominate XYZ title for the escrow services and the title insurance premium, the allocation of costs is to be split 50-50.

Regarding Addendum No. 1, unlimited access provided by me is something the seller can't agree to and I can't commit to. However, I can make myself available by appointment during the inspection contingency period. I'm pleased to do this.

Lastly, the sellers have informed me that they do not want at this time to be presented offers that come in less than $275,000. You may want to reconsider yours, if only to save time and effort."

Good to hear from you.

This e-mail you have sent to me from the agent who submitted your offer is typical of real estate agents who are trained to sell houses to owner occupants.

This agent has little to no experience with the expenses for turning a damaged property back to the market for lending funding.

All of the items in this e-mail are false and do not need to be the standard for accepting the offer.

By the way, this guy's title? At the end of the day his title and $5.00 gets a cup of coffee at Starbucks. You can't eat title. The person who puts the transaction together gets the respect.

At this point the property will not pass inspection for lender funding. They have the problem. If it had been priced correctly it would have already sold.

Let's look at your role here as the buyer.

The person who is considering spending his/her money is the CUSTOMER. Real estate agents are the same as a licensed car sales persons.

The person selling the property is the MERCHANT with inventory.

As a customer I EXPECT to be served if they want my money and or resources. I expect them "to kiss my feet" if they want my money.

I expect tremendous service if they want my money. I GET TO

CHOOSE WHERE I SPEND MY MONEY AND THEY NEED TO EARN IT!

That being said:

Most of your concerns here are because you are not prepared with what you need to perform.

All of this hesitation will go away when:

1. You have a data base of 200 investors, whom you have interviewed, with 3-day cash to close.
2. You have a smoking price accepted on the property and you are not just on the edge.
3. You have 30 real estate agents on your team who know how to go to battle for their customers and get the offer accepted by the seller.
4. You have properties that you have placed under contract, so well, that the other investors with cash are fighting to buy them from you.

Now you will be calling the shots and not the listing agent.

How would DONALD TRUMP handle it? TO BATTLE!

It is a terrific day!

Coach Bret Ehlers

Bret,

For the property we last discussed with the appraisal at 325,000, I spoke to the listing agent and he said that is based on the current condition of the home and that is price they are looking to sell it for. Based on that difference I'm concluding that this may not be a good deal.

Please let me know your thoughts.

We don't want to throw this property out, yet. We need to reduce your expenses to rehab the property in order to increase the offer to the seller and give you a profit.

We can do this with an extended 180 day closing. There are no correct or incorrect terms for this transaction. The contract will need to meet the needs of the property, the seller and you.

Having a listing agent in the middle of a seller involved transaction can make it more difficult. The agent is afraid of losing his/her commission. Very few real estate agents understand the process of legally protecting the seller and their property. When anyone is uneducated or afraid they say "no".

In my approach with the listing agent, the first thing I want to know is the motivation driving the sale?

Secondly, will the seller participate in seller financing.

This interview is in the "New Listing Agent Script".

Ask what the seller needs to accomplish first BEFORE you say anything about what you are going to do.

Here are some bullet points we could discuss with the agent for purchasing the property:

I'M GLAD YOU ASKED

1. The Buyer will purchase the property and close at the Title Company with the seller. (Closing Attorney).
2. The Buyer will have three days to inspect the property after signed acceptance of the offer by the seller.
3. The Buyer will purchase the property as is.
4. The Buyer will make monthly payments to the seller's escrow company for this agreement.
5. The existing financing will remain in place on the property up to 180 Days and the closing date.
6. The Seller's escrow company will send payments directly to the mortgage company, for principle, interest, taxes and insurance.
7. The Buyer will be given immediate possession of the property upon signed acceptance of this offer. The transaction time line will begin once the buyer is given access to the property.
8. As a favor to the seller the buyer will dispose of unwanted items and trash after the seller has taken all desired items.
9. The buyer would be responsible for the maintenance and repairs on the property during this agreement.
10. The Buyer will perform the needed repairs to prepare the property for the buyer's loan inspection and funding.
11. The buyer may assign this agreement.
12. The purchase price of the property will be the remaining balance of the unpaid mortgage which shall not exceed $75,000.00. The loan balance will be verified prior to the Buyer accepting the terms of the agreement.
13. The seller will be responsible for the listing contract.
14. Buyer and Seller will pay typical split closing costs.
15. The closing date will be before or on the last business day of the following month of the 180 days after the offer is accepted by the seller.
16. This agreement would be officially executed by the real estate attorney at the Title Company to include all protections and provisions of our mutual agreement.

There are many more possibilities depending on the needs of the seller. I am glad you contacted me before you threw out this property. It is not a sure thing but an alternative offer to present.

I will look forward to doing a conference call with you and the listing agent.

It's a terrific day!

Coach Bret Ehlers

Good Morning Bret,

This email is from another agent we chose for the 34th street property. We are trying to figure out if we (Nannette and Aaron) are not on the same page with the realtors, as them understanding we are investors that would be wholesaling this property. Please provide guidance on our next steps with the agent and/or with our buyers. We understand there will be closing costs, taxes, fees, etc., which is built into our "Best Offer strategy". Should we specify to the agent our desire is to get the contract in place with our contingencies and the end buyer will split the costs of closing or is there a better solution?

"I wanted you to see a few different options for the non-recurring closing costs amounts when you or the seller pay for them, or you split the cost on some are all. Obviously, the more you pay for the more attractive the offer. It is common to split some costs/fees or have the seller pay. With your offer being Approx. 10% below asking, these are some things to consider. I'll call you tomorrow to talk about it. These are only estimates of the actual costs."

This real estate agent is a retail agent and in bed with the seller's agent.

The transfer tax should be paid by the seller NOT you, the buyer.

I want to encourage you to carefully study the instructions which are attached in the "RE Broker Job Interview".

Does the agent meet the interview requirements?

In a job interview we want only the best working for our company, not someone who does not have our back.

In the corporate world they will interview 50 applicants if that is what it takes to find the right person for the job.

I am in an aggressive market just like yours. I always attempt to have the seller pay all of the transaction closing costs.

75% of the time they accept.

The offer is about your personal business safety with the offer; not what is best for the seller's safety.

You need an agent that has enough expertise to go to battle for you, get their job done, and make sure your offer is accepted.

They are to be on your team; not the sellers team.

Once you implement your real estate success systems you will have a greater ease with the real estate agents.

As for the margins in California, we are going to do a reverse and back out the costs and expenses from the ARV first.

The transactions costs will be reduced as long as you have your systems in place.

Using the standard 50% Fix and Flip formula, you have repairs, closing and holding costs, which are not going away.

1. Cost of Repairs. You can reduce these costs when you have the right material suppliers and a great and efficient contracting team in place.

This will make the numbers tighter and more competitive in your offer.

2. Closing and holding costs are typically 10% of (ARV) After Repair Value. When you pay cash you can reduce the holding costs.

Other investors who better manage these costs will be more competitive against you if they have streamlined their construction and holding costs.

In addition to reducing your construction, holding and acquisition costs how good are you at presenting alternate solutions to buy properties?

With certain transactions we can eliminate the majority of closing costs to give these expenses back to the seller. This is why you must have all of your systems in place and gather all of the information on the "Property Information Worksheet".

My expertise will be used to help with your offers. This is why we are working together.

You will want to engage each step with your business this week.

Let me know how I can help before our next appointment.

It's a terrific day!

Coach Bret Ehlers

My agent doesn't want to submit my "low ball offer".

What do I do?

Wow look at all of the properties with the High Ball asking prices LOL. If the real estate agents are accusing you of low ball offers then GOOD FOR YOU! That means you are following the investor's formulas to flip a property. After all, do you want to pay too much for a property and end up losing a lot of money because you cannot cover the expenses?

Here is the good news. No matter the offer price or the amount of earnest money, the agent is required by state law to present any and all offers. You will find some agents have no problem breaking the law and will not submit your offer. With bank owned properties and HUD properties there is not much we can do to fight the illegal actions of the listing agents.

The banks do not want to sell to investors if it can be avoided. They are looking to rip off some poor consumer with an overpriced property that will not pass a lender's own inspection criteria to give funding.

It is easier to have an offer presented on a property where a private seller has a listing agreement. Your buyer's agent places the offer with the listing agent and then you can present a copy of the offer directly to the seller. You are now assured the seller received your offer. You will not be able to do this with bank owned or HUD properties.

Typically, when a bank owned or HUD property comes to the market they are attempting to get as close to market value as possible. They want to sell to an owner occupant. Of course that same bank will not fund the property because of the property condition and situation.

This is why investors with cash will end up buying these properties. After the repairs are completed, the property will pass the inspection for a bank loan. Sometimes the banks and HUD have some good deals right from the start. Many times you will get the good deals on the aged property listings that did not sell when the property was first listed on the MLS.

Next time the real estate agents accused you of low ball offers here are some responses for you to use.

1. The bank has grossly over-valued this property for their High Ball asking price. Due to the condition of the property and the inability for the property to pass a funding inspection I am placing my offer at the accurate offer price.

2. My strategy is to purchase the property at the correct price so the property will pass a lenders inspection and appraisal for you to resell it for me after the repairs are completed.

3. You want to have the property properly priced for you to resell it don't you? Please place the offer I have given you.

If a real estate agent will not place the offer, have one of your other hundred agents that you have interviewed place the offer.

To Your Success

It is a terrific day!

Coach Bret Ehlers

How much earnest money do I have to give?

Earnest money is about fulfilling contract law not showing how strong we are with our offer.

Earnest money for bank owned or HUD properties will generally need to be more than $100. You will need to decide if you are willing to risk more than $1000 with your offer.

The Banks and HUD have added their own contract as an addendum to the State real estate contract. This action negates the state contract and requires you to perform as per the bank or HUD contract if you want to place an offer.

I recommend that you add your own addendum to their contract that states you will only provide the actual earnest money funds upon acceptance of your offer. Submit a copy of your earnest money check with your offer.

Remember: Hard money or loans are not cash. Make your offer contingent on the financing if you are unable to have cash in a couple of days.

To Your Success

It is a terrific day!

Coach Bret Ehlers

I was curious where I can find the resources for writing up and submitting offers. I feel I am able to do the math well, but when it comes to filling out the paper work, I would like to be more educated!

I am pleased with the work that you are doing to acquire a profitable property. Here are some pointers on contract basics.

I am going to attach a boiler plate doc, to this communication. It will include a simple "Standard Purchase Agreement" which is a two page document and a couple of other contracts that I use to control the real estate.

NOTE: Should you be working with a real estate broker or agent, by law they must use the "State Approved, Real Estate Purchase Contract".

Be sure to give your offer to the agent in writing. Use your "Simple Standard Purchase Agreement". You never want the agent telling you they did not know you wanted a certain item in your contract. Have It In Writing. The agent will transfer your information into their required contract.

Before you sign the agent's contract you must read the contract in full to make sure ALL items you want in the transactions are included and ALL items that you want eliminated from the contract are deleted.

Never place more than $100 in earnest money with your offer.

When you are purchasing real estate where an agent is not involved you do not need to use their State approved contract for the transaction. I use a simple two page agreement which is attached.

Here are the basics we write in the "Standard Purchase Agreement"

The names of all involved parties.

The agreed conditions between the parties.

Inspection contingencies for 14 business days that allow us to walk away from the property should we find repairs that make the property undesirable.

A beginning and ending date for the agreement.

The signature line with signatures of all involved parties.

$1 in earnest money to satisfy contract law.

You will have some properties that have contingencies you will want to include that would be specific to that property. I always do my time contingencies in business days to buy me a couple extra days.

If you are given someone else's contract, it is perfectly fine to red line anything in their contract you do not like, and have it deleted. Just because they wrote it down does not mean we have to agree to it in the contract. This includes real estate agent contracts.

You can also place additional terms in an addendum page at the end of the agreement to include items that are important to you in the transaction. This would also be true of contracts prepared by real estate agents and brokers.

I look at it from two angles. Is the property really worth the terms the seller wants or am I willing to live within the guidelines of the contract that they want to have? That should get you started.

To Your Success

It is a terrific day!

Coach Bret Ehlers

I found a great prospect for flip or wholesale. I contacted the heir. They are on board but cannot afford an attorney to get them in control of the property to sell to me and allow me or my agent access to the bank. The father died intestate. It is in preforclosure and needs to be shorted. Is it worth it for me to work with an attorney on this one? Should I take the risk? We are looking at minimum potential profit 50K on the fix and flip; probably more and maybe 20K on a wholesale. House needs everything and is in a very hot area. I am also a licensed broker. Also will a short sale expose the heir to tax liability?

To die 'Intestate' is where an individual died without a Legal Will or Living Family Trust.

The property and the assets of the individual are now under the control of a court-appointed executor. The assets of the deceased will be sold to pay any past financial liabilities to creditors and any Probate Taxes that are due. If there are proceeds remaining from the sale of the estate it will be dispersed to those parties that may be deemed as beneficiaries of the deceased's estate.

The Probate laws of each state vary. If you feel this is a viable real estate possibility you will want to contact your real estate attorney for instructions in pursuing this property based on the probate laws of your state.

To Your Success

It is a terrific day!

Coach Bret Ehlers

(By the way, everyone who is reading this needs to protect your family and estate with a Living Family Trust. Not just for your assets but for the protection of your young children. If something happens to you and you have no prior direction for your children, the State can seize your children and place them in foster care even though you have capable family who could care for them.

You want to have prior directions for how emergencies with your health are to be handled. If you do not have these directions in place, other people will be making the decision for your life and you will have no control. $500 will establish a Living Family Trust.)

I'M GLAD YOU ASKED

I am new to investing and unclear as to what to think about the description portion of this MLS listing.

"Investors must perform inspections prior to submitting an offer. Offers should be accompanied by EMD, and no contingencies, nor inspection periods permitted to investors. All offers should be accompanied by proof of funds, or PQ."

Am I looking for cheese where there is none or are my dispositions in the right direction?

Is this something I should look deeper into?

And what is a PQ? EMD?

By law real estate brokers and agents must submit ANY AND ALL OFFERS. By law they cannot dictate what or how you create your offer.

Now, in reality, the brokers and agents have no problem breaking the law. They will dictate what they want in the offer and it will never make it to the seller if the listing agent does not like the offer.

PQ = Prequalification – they want you to be preapproved for a loan.

EMD = Earnest Money Deposit

The first concern is to make sure that you and your money are safe.

Second, we will appease the agents to get the offer in front of the seller. No need, as the good book says: "Kicking against the ...." Perhaps I should have used: "Casting our pearls before swine".

Need a proof of funds letter? You can get one. Contingencies are a normal course of all business.

All of us need to be in solution mode. My mentor, Steve, 30 years ago, taught me one of my most valuable lessons. "Ehlers, don't ever again tell me you have a problem! You only have solutions to get the desired outcome".

To Your Success

It is a terrific day!

Coach Bret Ehlers

We are considering buying city condemned properties that may have had meth labs in them. Not fit for habitation until completely cleaned up. Do you have any experience with meth or grow lab clean ups?

Aaah! Meth and grow houses. I'm reminded of an old 70's pop song. Take a trip and never leave the farm. LOL, Just Kidding.

There is a property address meth disclosure that is available on most public records. The biggest difficulty to overcome is the public's perception of a health risk even when the property has been correctly decontaminated and rebuilt. Because of the public fear you will have trouble selling the property unless it is deeply discounted.

The educated public is aware of this property demise. They will be looking for a bargain. That means you will need to purchase the property at a substantially greater discount than we normally need when fixing and flipping a property. Every State and County has different regulations for the proper decontamination (abatement) procedures. You will need to contact the governing jurisdiction where the property is located for the requirements and needed permits.

Be sure to use licensed experts to do the decontamination procedures for you. This is not a transaction where you want to circumvent the system.

To Your Success

It is a terrific day!

Coach Bret Ehlers

CHAPTER 3 PROPERTY ANALYSIS

We wanted to know if we should go ahead with the purchase of this house if we aren't going to make 20% profit. It will be about $20k on a $140-145k ARV. Yesterday Paul's system told us you don't do the deal unless you make $30k. So we are just confused. We are having a hard time finding deals that are 50% of ARV in our area. So this one house would get us on the path to paying off some or our debt but we don't want to break the "rules" and then have a disaster happen and then we didn't follow the system and get more in debt.

Just wondered what your thoughts were and whether we should keep trying to pursue this deal.

There are plenty of deals available everywhere and you can make 20% without a 50% of ARV offer.

You have a very good question of discounting our profit.
It is all about safety, time and money. This transaction should take no more than 90 days from acquisition to sale and your payday.
That is three months. At 20% of $140 K you should clear $28,000.00 as long as your construction numbers are accurate and you have no hiccups. If you divide that amount by three months it pays you $9333.33 per month. A good income to get started.

At 15% of $140 you would make $21,000.00 which pays you $7000 a month. Not bad but a loss of $2300.33 dollars per month or a loss of $6901.00. What happens should you have a water problem you did not consider in your construction costs?

If you were buying real estate in LA, California where the property ARV begins at $450 and you discounted the profit to $15%, you still make $67,500.00. Because of the higher ARV you have a greater profit spread to work with should there be a difficulty.

You have less room to make a mistake with $140,000 ARV.

There is nothing confusing. At the end of the day what is your Risk vs. Reward?

Typically we get frustrated with real estate because we have not done the work to speak with and interview five 'For Sale By Owner' properties or RE agents per hour each day and we do not have our systems in place. When we have almost no choices we try to squeeze blood out of a transaction instead of GREEN, because that is all we have to work with.

I love a clip from the movie "Tommy Boy" on Youtube. It is the diner clip. It is sooo good. I encourage you to watch it this weekend.

Have a great 4th. After the holiday let's get your systems up and running and fill the pipeline.

Talk Soon.

It's a terrific day!
Coach Bret Ehlers

Can you please explain how a short sale actually works?

To control and secure a short sale before it is listed with a real estate agent you will need to:

Continue to contact everyone who knows who you are. Let them know that you buy real estate and help people with difficult real estate situations.

For little, to no, investor competition, call the 'For Sale By Owner' properties which are on NOD lists, 'For Sale By Owner' marketing in your area and vacant properties. Use the FSBO and Landlord scripts.

Place the property under contract with the seller using the Non-Exclusive option.

Have a loss mitigation company negotiate and complete the short sale for the seller. Some Loss Mitigation companies may require $2000 up front from the investor to initiate the process. Use experienced professionals to perform the short sales. Your time is too valuable to do this action.

Once the short sale amount has been approved by the bank, purchase the short sale property from the seller, through the bank, IF the short sale amount follows the Flipping Formulas. If the approved short sale amount is less than the Flipping Formula you can still make a nice profit by:

Working with your mortgage broker to access your "Buyer Incubation System" for a "Loan Ready" retail, owner occupant buyer. With your "Shell Entity" wholesale your Non-Exclusive option to another cash investor to pay you.

Place the Seller into your credit repair resources to help them begin their new financial life. As Coach Bell says, "Rinse and Repeat".

Actions For The Seller:

Once the NEO has been signed by the seller, have them place all unnecessary items in storage during the short sale negotiation period for an easier move when the short sale is approved.

Benefits To The Seller:

Stop collector harassment.

Live in the house for free during the negotiation.

Possible cash for keys to the seller up to $2500.

Your team will be doing all of the work for the seller.

You will help the seller to find an affordable, new place to live.

This could be another financial possibility for you.

Seller Financed home.

An investor in your data base with rentals,

To Your Success

It is a terrific day!

Coach Bret Ehlers

What is the best way to determine the ARV?

Great Question! COMPS ARE SOLD PROPERTIES ONLY!!! NOT PENDING OR ACTIVE LISTING.

When determining your final ARV you cannot use the electronic websites such as Zillow, Tulia or ACTIVE LISTINGS from agents, etc. These are just guesstimates.

The only accurate info is the recent SOLD PROPERTY comps from the MLS system and some States which have the sold info at the County Recorder's office, such as Florida. States like Utah are non-disclosure states and do not have the sold info available to the public, so we only have the MLS to determine value. That is why it is so critical when the agent is excited about sending you a property that they also send you a half dozen distressed sold comps and a half dozen regular sold comps, to verify the value of the property.

When you receive the comps you can assess the (ARV) After Repair Value of the subject home in about 30 seconds. The critical information needed from the comps the agent has sent, will be the square footage of the sold properties and how long it took to sell the property at the selling price. This is referred to as the (DOM) Days On Market and the year the property was built.

Write down the sold prices from the most expensive to the least expensive. I am looking for a compression of the numbers or the most amount of sold prices that are closest together. Eliminate the most expensive sold and the least expensive sold property. Eliminate the sold numbers where the square footage exceeds the square footage of your subject property by over 150 sq. ft. If your property is 2000 sq. ft. then I will eliminate all sold comps that exceed 2150 sq. ft. or, are less than 1850 sq. ft. At a later time we can calculate a neighborhood price per square foot when our offer is accepted. We are doing a quick 30 second decision.

Now look for the prices that are closest together which are similar to the property you are considering for an offer. Let's say the compression of the final comp numbers are $147K, $149K, $153K, $155K, $159K and $161K. Now I am going to look at the DOM. If the $155K and $161 took 120 days to sell, those two comps will not work for us and they are eliminated. We need to sell the property in 30 days after the repairs are completed. Now, I am going to consider my marketing strategies and the psychology of the buying public. Mentally, the public will look at the numbers of $153K and $155K as being a $160K price point. By choosing the $147K and $149K numbers the price mentally appears to be substantially lower than the $153 price, even though it is only $4000 dollars. I will be selecting the $145K as my After Repair Value to be just a little lower than the competition. If I have tighter completion in the market I would select the $149K as the ARV. It is still under the mental barrier of $150K.

30 seconds is up. We are done with the evaluation. You will be evaluating dozens of properties each week and you cannot afford to take much time making a decision. You need to get your offers submitted quickly before someone else beats you to the punch.

To Your Success

It is a terrific day!

Coach Bret Ehlers

I understand that the Zestimates from Zillow are usually way off. However, can I still use the "sold" comps on Zillow to calculate my ARV in a particular area?

Any source that provides verifiable sold property data is a good source for determining the After Repair Value (ARV). Many counties also provide this information to the public unless they are a non-disclosure State. Many of the counties in Florida provide an online sold data comp system to the public that is equal to the real estate agents Multiple Listing Service (MLS).

The only accurate info is the recent SOLD PROPERTY comps from the MLS system and some States which have the sold info at the County Recorder's office, such as Florida. States like Utah are non-disclosure states and do not have the sold info available to the public so we only have the MLS to determine value. That is why it is so critical that when the agent is excited about sending you a property, they also send you a half dozen distressed sold comps and a half dozen regular sold comps to verify the value of the property.

When you receive the comps you can assess the (ARV) After Repair Value of the subject home in about 30 seconds.

The critical information that is needed from the comps the agent has sent will be: The square footage of the sold properties and how long it took to sell the property at the selling price. This is referred to as the (DOM) Days On Market and the year the property was built.

Write down the sold prices from the most expensive to the least expensive. I am looking for a compression of the numbers or the most amount of sold prices that are closest together.

Eliminate the most expensive sold and the least expensive sold property. Eliminate the sold numbers where the square footage exceeds the square footage of your subject property by over 150 sq. ft. If your property is 2000 sq. ft. then I will eliminate all sold comps that exceed 2150 sq. ft. or are less than 1850 sq. ft. At a later time we can calculate a neighborhood price per square foot when our offer is accepted. We are doing a quick 30 second decision.

Look for the prices that are closest together which are similar to the property you are considering for an offer. Let's say the compression of the final comp numbers are $147K, $149K, $153K, $155K, $159K and $161K. Now, I am going to look at the DOM. If the $155K and $161 took 120 days to sell, those two comps will not work for us and they are eliminated. We need to sell the property in 30 days after the repairs are completed. So, I am going to consider my marketing strategies and the psychology of the buying public. Mentally, the public will look at the numbers of $153K and $155K as being a $160K price point. By choosing the $147K and $149K numbers the price mentally appears to be substantially lower than the $153 price even though it is only $4000 dollars. I will be selecting the $145K as my After Repair Value to be just a little lower than the competition. If I have tighter completion in the market I MAY select the $149K as the ARV. It is still under the mental barrier of $150K.

30 seconds is up. We are done with the evaluation!

You will be evaluating dozens of properties each week and you cannot afford to take much time in making a CORRECT decision. You need to get your offers submitted quickly before someone else beats you to the punch.

To Your Success

It is a terrific day!

Coach Bret Ehlers

What is an easy and fast way to estimate the cost to replace flooring in a house?

Is there and average cost per sq.ft. that includes labor and material that can be used?

Also what is a quick way to calculate the number of square feet that will be needed without having to get out the tape measure?

You will be using a large amount of flooring in each house you renovate. In fact, flooring is one of the single largest expenses in your construction costs.

Hard surface, fired products such as ceramic tile and wood is measured by the square foot and carpet is measured by the sq. ft. and also by the square yard. A square yard is nine sq. ft.

The cost of the material and labor is priced by the sq. ft. or sq. yard for materials and labor. For material and labor you should be able to purchase and install very good quality product for about $3.00 per sq. ft.

You may have extra labor expenses on your job for removal of the old floor coverings or special decorative trim work.

For quick room calculations measure the length times the width to get the square footage of the room to be covered.

Take your net measurements and add 8% to accommodate the extra material needed to seam, cut and trim the materials to the room size.

I would love to give you a quick measure technique. You will need to get out the tape measure.

In the beginning, you can use the square footage posted in the MLS listings or the information given to you by the owner. It is close enough to place an offer.

Now, let's place some offers today

To Your Success

It is a terrific day!

Coach Bret Ehlers

CHAPTER 4 PROPERTY REPAIRS

Hi Bret. Thanks for talking to us. We are excited about our property….. but nervous!

How do we work with contractors?

Congratulations on your property.

We have all heard the Contractor horror stories. Here are some things we have learned to implement in our business. Some of the items were learned by our hard knocks. LOL

Not funny when you are having the experience.

CONTRACTOR SELECTION:

1. Licensed!!
2. Insured:
    a. You need to be on the contractor's policy as an additional insured. First Payee.
3. You must itemize each item that is to be repaired on your property:
    a. Create floor plan sketch.
    b. Create finish schedule for every nail that needs repaired in each room.
    c. On your spec sheet write down what is to be performed on each surface. Ceiling, floor, walls and each opening.
    d. Identify the quality of materials and workmanship to be used.
    e. Take pictures of each room and the work to be performed in that room.
4. Supply the above itemized information to THREE Contractors for them to prepare a competitive bid to submit to you.
5. All Contractor bids must be itemized and in writing.

THE FOLLOWING IS CRITICAL:

1. Have a signed contract with the itemized work to be performed by the contractor.
2. Do Not Pay the contractor up front. Only pay when the work is completed.
3. You will buy the materials and have the contractor sign for them.
4. If the contractor is not financially strong enough to wait 30 days for payment, he is a risk to you.
5. Make sure you only pay the contractor in exchange for a signed and notarized lien release from every finger that touched your project.

There are several things you will need for your personal protection and liability from licensed and unlicensed contractors. The "Hold Harmless" provisions are generally included in a sub-contractor contract or agreement.

Here are the following liabilities from which you will need to protect yourself and business. You will be gathering a series of contracts and other information.

1. Number one is protection from the government. You must prove the contractor is not an employee. You do not want the contractor to claim employee status after the work is completed and they have been paid. You Will Lose.

    a. Have the contractor sign the "Independent Contractor Agreement for Direct Sellers". This is a contract that the independent contractor signs only once and you keep this in your files to prove you did not hire him/them as an employee.
    b. You must get a copy of their social security card or a document that has their name and SS#. This can be a W-2, past 1099 or tax return. You will need to have them complete an IRS form W-9 and file a 1099 for each

person who does work for you which exceeds $650 annually. Do Not Pay Cash under the table.
2. Second is protecting yourself from the services and damage done by the independent, uninsured contractor. (Not a good idea . Insurance just is not that expensive for a small time operator). Do not add them to your insurance as an additional insured.
    a. You will need them to sign the "Independent Contractor Services Agreement". Item 15 gives you the "Hold Harmless" indemnification. This contract will be modified for each project the independent contractor performs. Should an item in the contract not apply, just delete it from the contract before they sign it.
3. Third. You need to add an amendment for every nail that you want to have repaired on every project. This needs to include exact materials, brand of fixture, quality of work and the drop dead date they will be completed with the project. You should also include a "Liquidated Damages" clause where they pay you for every day the project is not completed beyond the completion date.
4. Never authorize a change order until you have the scope of work and price, in writing, from the contractor.
5. Fourth. NEVER pay the contactor any money up front until the work is completed and inspected as per the amendments to the contract. You pay for the materials up front directly to the supplier.
6. Lastly, you need to obtain a lien release for every finger that touched your project in exchange for your payment to the contractor.

Follow these instructions and you will never have a financial problem with the contractors.

It's a terrific day!

Coach Bret Ehlers

Independent Contractor Agreement for Direct Sellers

This Agreement is made this_____ day of _____, 199 by and between DIRECT SELLER of COUNTY, STATE (hereinafter Contractor), and OWNER, of COUNTY, STATE (hereinafter Owner).

WITNESSETH:

Whereas, Contractor is, and has been, in the business as a sole proprietor of selling or soliciting the sale of products in the homes of various individuals; and

Whereas, Owner has need for such services in HIS/HER/ITS business of selling PRODUCT;

NOW, THEREFORE, the parties hereto do hereby agree and contract as follows:

1. Contractor agrees to sell PRODUCT for Owner by seeking sales of the PRODUCT in the homes of various individuals. This work will be done by Contractor as an independent contractor, and *not* as an employee.

2. Owner agrees to pay Contractor a commission for sales made at the rate of X percent (X%) of the gross sales prices for the products sold and paid for by purchasers. Contractor hereby acknowledges that no other compensation is payable by Owner, and that all of Contractor's compensation will depend on the sales made by Contractor and will not be related, one way or the other, to the number of hours worked by Contractor. No commissions are payable until the purchaser has paid for the product sold. Owner shall remit to Contractor the commission earned on a sale within one calendar week following receipt from the purchaser of payment in full for the product.

3. Contractor shall provide Contractor's own supplies necessary or advisable to perform the work in a workmanlike

manner, except that Owner will supply Contractor with forms for finalizing each sale and reporting sales and remitting proceeds to Owner.

4. Contractor shall have no obligation to work any particular hours or a particular amount of hours and shall further have the right to refuse to sell PRODUCTS offered by Owner as Contractor.

5. Contractor shall have no obligation to perform any services other than the sale of PRODUCT and related activities associated with the sale of PRODUCT.

6. Contractor retains the right to contract for similar services with other individuals and other businesses.

7. Contractor agrees to perform the sales in a manner in accord with ordinary business customs and good taste.

8. Owner agrees that neither Owner, nor Owner's agents or representatives, shall have any right to control or direct the details, manner or means by which Contractor accomplishes the results of Contractor's sales.

9. Contractor shall have the right to subcontract and sales and, if Contractor chooses to subcontract and sale, or to use employees to complete any sale or any part of it, then Contractor agrees to see that such work is performed in accordance with the terms of this Agreement.

10. Contractor agrees to secure the necessary licenses for operation of Contractor's business, and to conduct such business in full compliance with all applicable laws, codes, and regulations.

11. Each party shall have the right to cancel this Agreement upon thirty (30) days written notice, hand-delivered or sent by return receipt mail to the other party's last known address.

12. Contractor agrees to obtain an employer identification number from the Internal Revenue Service and to comply with all tax laws applicable to the operation of a business such as Contractor's, including, but not limited to, the reporting of all gross receipts therefrom, as income from the operation of a

business, the payment of all self-employment taxes, compliance with all employment tax requirements for withholding on any employees used by Contractor, and compliance with State employment Workmen's Compensation laws. Contractor hereby acknowledges that he/she will not be treated as an employee with no respect to services under this agreement for Federal tax purposes.

    13.   This Agreement shall be construed in accordance with the laws of the State of _____.

WHEREFORE, the parties have set their hands and seals the day and year first above written.

_____(SEAL)

WITNESS   CONTRACTOR

ATTEST: ss.   XXX CORPORATION, OWNER

                                        By:_____ ____(SEAL)

SECRETARY   President

What is your reason for not using some of the larger insurance companies?

I have had great success working with independent insurance agents.

They are able to shop rates and coverages with multiple insurance carriers for the best price and services.

Whether you have buy and hold or rehab properties you will want to have your agent shop for a Landlord / Tenant Policy with a tenant damage rider for your real estate.

It should only cost about $450 - $650 a year for the bread and butter properties we buy.

I purchase a separate policy for each property. I inform the agent that we have acquired the property and we will be getting the property occupant ready so it is understood that the property is vacant during the repairs.

If you have a seller finance property you will want to convert the owner's occupant policy to the Landlord / Tenant policy with a tenant damage rider.

Have the owner place you on the policy as an additional insured with two party payee and dual signature endorsement on the check or to the trustee that is officiating over the finances and bill pay service.

Should the owner's occupancy policy be more expensive than the $650 annual premium, replace the owner's current insurance company with a more competitive carrier.

We have a $1,000.00 deductible and if the repair is $1600.00 we pay it out of our pocket. I do not place a claim with the insurance company.

Insurance is for a catastrophe!

Do not nickel and dime your insurance carrier for repairs or they will shut off your coverage. With the national insurance registry all carriers have access to your insurance history.

If you have frequent claims you will not be able to get coverage. In 36 years I have placed one claim for tenant damage that was $29,000.00.

Be sure to know the destructive events that are included in your policy. Breaking or freezing water pipes, floor or water damage from inside and outside of the structure, snow, hail and wind damage, roof damage, what if your tree falls on the house or neighbor's car, earthquake, break-ins with vandalism and what is covered if someone stumbles over their dog while walking on your property and tries to sue you.

I deliberately insure each property separately so that it does not drag the rest of the real estate portfolio into the review of the subject property.

Always get in writing, the coverage the agent represents with the policy. Never believe the word of the insurance company unless it is in writing. If you have a conversation over the phone be sure to demand an e-mail follow up from the carrier's representative for the commitments that were made in the telephone conversation.

I will not use State Farm, Farmers, Farm Bureau or All State. We have had success with Allied, USF&G (if they are still in business), Hartford, Progressive, Metlife, and American Family. American Family has become more restrictive with their policy coverage in the last 3 years.

Be sure to interview several American Family and independent agents before selecting with whom you will work. The agent makes a huge difference in the service level you will receive from the carrier.

NEVER HOLD AN UNINSURED PROPERTY!

To Your Success

It is a terrific day!

Coach Bret Ehlers

I am going to be looking at a property that has had fire damage to it. Before I look I want to have a template as to what to look for in the property.

I realize that fire can cause not just the initial damage in what is burned but also a residual damage as to what will smell continually. Do I have to take everything down to the stud? Who should I be in contact with. The city? Flood/restoration people?

It can be these properties in my view that can have the biggest benefit in that there is a perceptual disjoint in what it will cost to fix. If I can pick up this property for a price that the market that does not have perfect info sees, then its great if it is in my favor.

Again, I understand we are in the solution business. Information is key. Any help on this matter would be appreciated.

Thanks again,

When you are new to the investing business, the fastest and safest resource to determine expenses on a fire damage property is to have the listing agent obtain the insurance repair quote. The quote will typically be lower than the actual repairs to the property. Add 20% to the insurance quote to cover your costs.

You will also want to know who received the check from the insurance company and the amount of the check. Use the insurance money as part of the negotiation for the final purchase price.

All you need to do now, is calculate the rehab formula and submit your offer with a 14 business day inspection contingency.

Once your offer has been accepted have THREE contractors who specialize in fire restoration, meet you at the property. Give them the insurance repair list for a competitive quote.

They will know how to handle the issues of the smoke and heat penetration and elimination of the lingering smoke smells. Use their expertise to work with the City for the needed compliance and permits.

Surround yourself with experts to become an expert and stay safe.

To Your Success

It is a terrific day!

Coach Bret Ehlers

> *I just put a contract on a home in which the interior drywall is covered in mold. It is a wood frame single family, and It appears like a previous investor was almost finished rehabbing the place but left after it flooded. My contractor believes the water damage was done intentionally, but regardless the basement, first floor & second has mold all on the walls (on the drywall). I know all this has to be replaced, but has anyone come across this before? My contractor says he is licensed with the EPA and can remove it, but i wonder if the wood framing needs to be sprayed or painted so the mold doesn't come back? And is there anything else I should be aware of? Thank you!*

Did your contractor tell you the mold was toxic black mold or is he making it sound worse than it is to charge you a premium?

The majority of mold that you will find in most houses is non-toxic surface mold.

The toxic mold found in properties, is due to a building design flaw, (in the 80's thru mid-90's) that was supposed to increase energy efficiency. Interior moisture from inside the house, from human habitation, showers and cooking is trapped between the interior and exterior walls with no ventilation for the moisture to evaporate. With the different temperatures between the exterior and interior walls this creates a stagnant environment to provide an excellent incubator for toxic mold growth. This construction technique is no longer used.

This subject property sounds like shower mold on a larger scale. All of us have had shower mold. The shower mold was easily remedied with bleach and water which killed the spores. You did not need to bring in a governmental agency approved, licensed contractor to repair your shower mold unless you live in California. (I am only kidding, California.)

You can have a testing lab inexpensively analyze the mold if you are concerned.

I am more concerned about the water leaks. Where did the water originate to do that much damage? Was there a winter freeze, pressure burst, tiny holes drilled into the pipes by a mad, evicted owner, or roof leaks?

After we strip the damaged area we do not want to do any repairs until the leaks are resolved and pressure tested, if the leaks were a plumbing issue.

The steps to repairing the damage:

1. Remove all of the damaged sheetrock that has been soaked in the water or has developed mold. The sheetrock will have wicked the water to a higher point than the actual flood level. Remove only the damaged sheetrock. Everything you are able to save makes you money on the rehab.

2. After the sheet rock and insulation has been removed, mix one part bleach and four parts water in a garden sprayer and heavily spray the studs that have mold and let dry completely.

    Be sure to have good ventilation during this procedure.

3. After the lumber has dried, seal the wood surface from odors and future mold growth with lacquer based Kilz before you install the new insulation and sheet rock.

    Be sure to have good ventilation during this procedure.

4. All you do now is mud, tape.

5. Prime all surfaces with lacquer based Kilz and paint the entire house with a latex base paint.

6. These steps will also take care of any lead based paint issues as well. All houses constructed up to 1979 have lead based paint.

Run your numbers and place an offer on this property!

To Your Success

It is a terrific day!

Coach Bret Ehlers

CHAPTER 5 INVESTMENT METHODS

Hello Brett, I watched a video about discounted real estate notes. Can you tell me if it's worth exploring?

Good Morning,

Discounted notes can be an excellent passive or active income source. Notes are a term for any type of financial paper which is secured by a physical asset.

In Real Estate, the note refers to a mortgage or real estate contract which is secured or collateralized by the real estate.

This instrument can be purchased from banks, investors, businesses, factors or private individuals. For immediate earnings you must purchase the note or contract for a discount from the face value amount of the original contract.

For example the bank gave the original borrower a loan for $100,000.00 which is secured by a note (mortgage) and a Deed of Trust which gives the lender the right to foreclose on the property and take the collateral which secured the loan in the event of non-payment by the borrower.

Now the bank wants to sell the note to recapture some of the money which was loaned to the original borrower. The note is for sale for $85,000.00. The person who purchases the note from the bank will have $15,000.00 immediate equity in the note and they now receive the original borrower's monthly payments which includes the interest on the original $100,000.00 mortgage. The note discount increases the return on the interest percentage of the original note. (ROI)

As the new note holder your risk is nonpayment from the original borrower. In the event of default by the borrower you will foreclose on the asset which secured the note and sell the real estate to reimburse you for the loan. When you obtain the property it could be trashed and the property value could be less than the note. As the note holder you could insure the property for damage to minimize your risk.

The new owner of the note must comply with the original contract terms to the borrower. You may have seen a letter in your mortgage statement envelope alerting you to the sale of your mortgage note to another bank or mortgage servicing company. Your original mortgage has been sold. The agreement for payments from your original mortgage does not change. The only change may be a new company name on your check and the address where you send your payments. I do not recommend paying your mortgage electronically. A paper trail will always prove your on-time payments to the note owner.

The note can be sold as many times as a buyer sees value in purchasing the note.

It's a terrific day!

Coach Bret Ehlers

I'M GLAD YOU ASKED

Can one purchase a mobile home and rent it out? The answer getting from parks state it is against the rules to rent out the mobile. Please help.

Bernie, in most states it is perfectly legal to buy a manufactured home in a park and rent the home to a tenant. I would contact one of the real estate attorneys you work with at your title company and ask them the laws for your State. I never trust someone who tells me something is against the law unless they provide me a written copy of the law. As the owner of a home in a park owned by someone else you are at risk. You cannot control the park ownership and lot rent increases. If you become unhappy with the park owners the expenses to move and reset your rental home will exceed $10,000.00. Buy the home cheap and receive a high rent payment from your tenant.

To Your Success

It is a terrific day!

Coach Bret Ehlers

CHAPTER 6 SELLING PROPERTIES

I'M GLAD YOU ASKED

Hi Bret, How can encourage competition amongst the buyers for the property we have under contract? Thanks for your help.

Good Morning,

It is time for your payday on this transaction. This is why you have been doing all of the interviewing to find the 30 investors with Cash.

You want to get as much money as you can for the property as a wholesaler.

It is not based on a percentage, but how good the job the wholesaler does in getting the property under contract at the right price, and having a huge database of rehab investors, with cash, who can place their money at the title company in 2 to 3 days, to fund and close.

When you have 30, 60, 100 plus investors, with cash, who can close in two to three days, you can expose the property to all of the investors, and let them know that whoever comes up with the most money for the property, and places the money at the title company in two to three days, gets it.

It is up to you to do a great job following the formula for placing the property under contact, at the right price, or NO ONE will buy it from you.

1. Calculate the Buying Formula for a cash purchase price offer. Include your wholesaling commission if you are not going to do the fix and flip.

2. Using the Flipping Formula, subtract the following costs from the (ARV) 30 day After Repair Value:

a. 20% of the ARV for your profit.

b. 10% of the ARV for your expenses.

c. Subtract the agent commission and transfer taxes for resale.

d. Subtract the construction costs from your contractor bid.

e. Subtract your wholesale commission.

f. Subtract the items above from the ARV to give you the maximum offer.

3. You need to buy the property for about half of the current After Repair Value, for cash, or the seller needs to leave their existing financing in place.

Here is the investor interview:

1. You can obtain cash resources and create a database of investors and buyers at the same time. When you adhere to the Buying Formula, you will be able to wholesale your properties to these investors. You want to have a database of dozens and dozens of investors who pay fast cash.

To find these cash buyers, start with the electronic and print classifieds in your area, and look under the following categories: (I also have a long list of seller websites if you need them.)

   a. Real estate wanted.

   b. Money to loan.

   c. Money wanted.

   d. Business opportunity.

   e. Bandit Signs you see in your community.

   f. Your local real estate investing club.

   g. Referrals.

2. Call each ad and interview the investor. Let them know you have seen their advertising and you want to know:

   a. Am I speaking with the principle?

   b. What types of properties do they purchase?

c. How far below market value do they need to purchase the property?

d. Do they cash to close at the Title Company in two to three days or, do they need to wait for funding?

e. Do they have a price cap for each property?

3. Attend the following events to meet investors with cash:

a. Trustee Sale.

b. Sheriff Sale.

c. Tax Lien or Tax Deed Auctions.

d. Other Auctions.

e. Introduce yourself to all of the participants who bid at the auctions. These are the people with cash, or they have access to cash.

f. Find out if they would purchase from you if you had the right transaction to meet their criteria.

g. Find out what they buy.

h. Find out the discounts they expect to have for their purchases.

i. Ask if they have cash or do they need to wait for funding.

j. How quickly can they provide funding to close at the Title Company or with the closing attorney?

4. Advertising for investors to call you can be posted in the following categories:

a. The Real Estate "for sale" and "for rent" section of the classifieds.

b. All of the categories previously listed in item 1.

Post the following ad copy for investors to call you:

FIXER FOR SALE - NEED FAST CASH

CALL (your name) TODAY   xxx-xxx-xxxx

When the investor responds to your ad you let them know that you place deep discounted properties under contract and sell the properties to local investors with cash. You ask them if they would like to be considered for these properties in the future.

You then conduct the same investor interview as above:

   a. Am I speaking with the principle?

   b. What type of properties do they purchase?

   c. How far below market value do they need to purchase the property?

   d. Do they have cash to close in two to three days at the Title Company or do they need to wait for funding?

   e. Do they have a purchase price cap on each property?

It is soon to be a really terrific day!$$$$$

Talk Soon.

Coach Bret Ehlers

Thanks, Bret! Do we put the price in the ad?

Good question about placing the price of your property in the ads!

I do not place the price in the ads. There are people who suggest you should place the price in the ads for pre-screening the buyers to keep them from calling you.

I market, to create curiosity and to get the phone to ring.

From the respondents to the ad, I glean all of the possibilities to make money by helping everyone who is serious, to purchase a home.

Even if your home does not work for them, you can make money between your transactions by getting that buyer "loan qualified" with your mortgage broker.

If you have not found the buyer a suitable property, give the lead to the real estate agents on your team. They will love you.

You can also become part of another investor's property transaction.

I want to see how I can help people, and by helping them buy a home, you are paid.

I am looking forward to hearing your progress.

It's a terrific day!

Coach Bret Ehlers

Hi Bret,

Once you purchase the property & it's not moving fast enough & goes over the 60 - 90 days. How should you handle the property to make a profit?

Thanks again

There are two critical elements I keep stressing to new investors.

Most don't believe me and prefer to trust the RE agents with bad numbers and information. After the real estate agents have gotten their commission they are gone and not to be available when the problems begin. I am the one that gets the calls to do damage control. I can do damage control but it is always going to be really painful.

So from my Soap Box, here we go.

Number One:

Be sure you absolutely know the 30 day After Repair Value (ARV).

Not the 60 day, not the 90 day: Only the price you can sell the property in 30 days after the repairs are completed.

Here is the time-line from the acquisition of the property to the sale and your payday:

a. The time-line begins when you close and acquire the property.

b. For every $40K in repairs, it should only take a GOOD contractor 30 days to have the repairs completed.

c. After the repairs are completed, the property is sold and closed in 30 days max.

With this example you should have your pay day in 60 days from beginning to end.

There are new investors who have falsified the real 30 day ARV and they are in big trouble!

Number Two:

Begin marketing for buyers NOW with your mortgage brokers, before you have a property. Every new investor with whom I work, who has waited until the property is repaired and ready for occupancy, has had difficulty getting it sold quickly.

I was on the phone this morning with a title officer in Texas for a student that has her home on the market for more than two months in a booming economy. This is a great home, well priced and still for sale. She offered to tell other students of this mistake. Texas is claimed to be a booming market. Their title office is having buyers drop out of escrow right and left because the banks are looking for every excuse to kill the loans. Over 50% of loan declines in the last quarter had 740 or above credit scores. She told me of the 800 scores that are not clearing underwriting to fund and close at their office.

There is soooo much competition from the real estate agents, other investors, and For Sale By Owners, for loan ready buyers. Should your buyer fall out of escrow and your beautiful home is off the market for the closing, what are you going to do for a backup for buyers who CAN close?

Having loan-ready buyers allows you to quickly engage in other transaction types.

In answer to your question of how to handle a property which is not selling, to enable you to receive a profit:

My recommendation is for you to implement your systems and actions NOW which will keep you from those mistakes in the future.

Like Grandma used to say before she died: "An ounce of prevention beats a pound of cure." I will add to her quote: "A pound of cure is going to be really painful."

Let me know how I can help you.

It is a terrific day!

Coach Bret Ehlers

CHAPTER 7 YOUR BUSINESS

Good afternoon Bret, We have forgotten to inquire on the steps that we need to take to transfer our business from Oklahoma to Colorado?!

You will need to establish a new State entity in Colorado for a business transfer. The name you have registered in Oklahoma may not be available in Colorado.

You should speak with your tax professional concerning keeping the Oklahoma entity and using it to do business in Colorado.

Some States may require you to register an out-of-State entity as a "Foreign Entity" in their State. In some states you will pay the same registration fee or more when you have a registered "Foreign Entity". You will need to find out the regulations in Colorado.

As for the company name in Colorado, if your name is taken: I prefer to base the company name from an available URL from Go Daddy.com. Now you will search to determine if the name is available with the State. This can usually be done online at the State website with instant results. When you have registered the name with the State, purchase the URL name at Godaddy for the company name.

Let me know how I can help.

It's a terrific day!

Coach Bret Ehlers

I'M GLAD YOU ASKED

Good morning Bret:

I need your help!!

We were about to close on our second house next week then my agent told me the buyers check bounce and he changed his mind. He doesn't want to buy the house anymore. He only give us $1000.00 and the other $1000.00 check bounced.

What should we do? We have the right to sue but it will cost me more than the first and second check. What do you recommend?

Thanks and God bless you

Here is the information for the termination letter:

Beyond this, you will want to engage a real estate attorney to continue the process.

It is my encouragement to keep it out of the courts. This is really expensive.

To _____ (name of broker) and _____ (Agent)

This is notice of intimidate termination of the listing agreement with _____ for the property located at :

This termination is due to the Broker / Agent violation and breech of the listing agreement contract as per the contract and the laws of the State of Pennsylvania and contract terms of the listing agreement.

Section 6 and line 67

Section 11 line 96-101

Section 17 155-158

and other sections of the contract which may have been violated.

We will be pursuing damages as per Philadelphia State Law.

Signage is to be removed from the property.

We will honor commissions on the names of prospective buyers which have been shown the property by _____ (name of broker) and _____ (Agent) or offers which have been submitted to date by other brokers.

The listing sign must be removed and the buyers list submitted to _____ (You) by _____, 201_ end of business day.

Regards

(You Name)

Company Entity

In the future you will want to include the following items in your listing agreement:

When listing your personal property for sale with a real estate broker / agent you need to include the following exclusions by addendum to the listing agreement:

1. You are going to market the property while it is listed with the agent in non MLS sources.
2. The real estate agent will have all of the signage on the property and they will be the only contact from the signs on the property.
3. Should you find the buyer to purchase the property before the real estate agent, you will close your transaction at the Title Company and pay no agent commission. You do not need an agent for the property closing. The Title Company or closing attorney will perform these services as part of the typical closing costs.
4. Your listing agreement will only be for 90 days. If you are not unhappy with the performance of the agent you can renew the listing for another 90 days. You should have had the property priced to sell in 30 days.
5. You may want to consider giving an additional 1% bonus to the buyer's agent who sells the property within the first 30 days. We all love extra incentives!

I believe in paying for performance - not doing the work for someone and paying them for non-performance.

It's a terrific day!

Coach Bret Ehlers

Bret,

Does it matter if we use our home address vs a UPS address for the LLC?

On the LLC, once created, I guess whatever it defaults to we'll deal with. No clue on the S vs the C corp benefit. Spoke to my accountant and he said I have to pay tax on any income that comes in???

If you disagree, can u guide me to someone who knows?

These are great questions.

My tax professionals have me working through an "S" Corp for the operating entity. This entity holds no assets. It is referred to as operating "Bare".

If the entity is sued there is nothing to seize. All funds are liquid in 60 seconds and strictly used for short term business and operating expenses and income.

You will want to speak with your business tax specialists to give you direction for your situation.

In the past 20 years only 15% of the accountants and CPA's that I have interviewed have passed the following interview question.

Franchise accounting companies are great for W-2 employees but not generally for sophisticated business tax law.

This is the interview question which will weed out the tax people who do not specialize in business and real estate tax law.

"How do I loan my paycheck to my Sub-Chapter "S" Corporation or single member Limited Liability Company (LLC) and deduct it?"

Where most new real estate investors also have current W-2 employment, this is a simple, in the middle of white, allowable tax benefit for you and your real estate business.

The following is a basic organization of the steps: (Of course you will want to utilize the services of your tax professional who understands these legal principles and knows your personal situation.)

1. You bring home your paycheck from your job.
2. You deposit it into your personal bank account.
3. You subtract all personal expense items from your paycheck.
4. You write a check for the remaining W-2 funds from your personal checking account to your business checking account.
5. The business has now received a loan from you, personally. (It is also referred to as owner's contribution.)
6. The business now has borrowed the funds which show as debt on the company accounting books. (We use QuickBooks Pro accounting software.)
7. You now pay for all of the business expenses from the money that has been loaned, by you personally, to the company. All of your expenses are business unless they are personal. All of the business expenses are deductible.
8. The company now shows a loss on the business and since the above entities are pass-through entities, you can take the losses from the business as personal deductions from your paycheck. It is so easy and legal.

You will always want to consult your own tax and legal professionals for your individual needs and situation.

This is what my business professionals have me do: (I think this is the third time I have mentioned this.)

Since I am not a tax professional I make sure I have the disclaimer, several times, in my communication concerning taxes. LOL

Talk Soon.

It is a terrific day to LEGALLY maximize the IRC.

Coach Bret Ehlers

Help! I can't seem to get it all done. What do I do?

You have begun the journey to a new life. You currently have some time wasting baggage that needs to be discarded if you are to move forward with your future. It may not be easy. How important is your dream of a new life?

Here are the steps my mentor taught me 28 years ago.

Write your dreams and goals of your new life at the top of an 8 1/2 x 11 sheet of paper.

Draw a line down the middle of the paper.

On the left side of the line write down all of your current time commitments: occupation, spiritual, personal, family, recreation, charity and other.

After you have written down all time commitments for each day, week, month and year look at your goals. You are now going to cross out each time waster that will not get you closer to reaching your goals.

For the time commitments that are left, rewrite those items on the right side of the line on your paper. Schedule the items on the right side of the page into your paper calendar for the next three months.

Now schedule the time for your real estate business. The following items are what you will be doing each day:

You should be able to speak with six to eight people per hour. If you have one hour a day you will be speaking with eight individuals.

Now, don't let anyone steal your future by stealing the time you have secured for your real estate business.

To Your Success

It is a terrific day!

Coach Bret Ehlers

Any tips for me?

Have you chosen to enjoy the success you envisioned when you decided to invest in real estate?

Here are some easy steps to keep you on your success track:

1) Hang around people whom you want to be like.

2) Consistency and Follow up is the Key for Long-Term Success.

3) Struggles can be part of the process.

4) Hard Work is part of the Game.

5) Model others that are actually doing real estate.

6) Follow through and don't quit.

To Your Success!

It is a terrific day!

Coach Bret Ehlers

In answer to your question I'm scared to make the phone call. I don't think I can answer the seller's questions. I just feel stupid.

Many people are a little afraid that they will appear to be uneducated or the fool, concerning real estate investing, if they are asked a question they cannot answer.

In Chapter 5 of the book "Think and Grow Rich" by Napoleon Hill, there is an account of a law suit that was won by Henry Ford. He won the suit on the precedent that he did not have to have all of the answers. HE ONLY NEEDED TO KNOW WHERE TO GET THE ANSWERS. That being said, here are a couple of simple tips to assist you:

1. The person asking the questions controls the conversation about the transaction. Learn to spend the conversation asking the seller questions about their needs and the situation with the real estate. I use the Sellers Information Worksheet.

2. When asked a question where you do not have the answer, all you need to say is, "That is a great question! I will be speaking with my associate and I will get back to you with the answer".

3. Or, when asked a question where you do not have the answer, all you need to say is, "We have a program for that. I will be speaking with my associate and we will make arrangements to get the details to you".

It is really simple to look the professional and be very wealthy, just like Henry Ford.

It is a terrific day!

Coach Bret Ehlers

In starting my investing business, what should my voicemail say?

I have listened to many student voice mail messages over the years.

I would like to share some tips on your recoded voice mail message:

(You will always want to use your personal voice mail message.)

1. The auto default electronic message does not represent you well.

2. If you have a strong accent, have someone record the voice mail message in your behalf. It is preferable to have a female voice. The reason for this is that Americans are terrible at listening. This is not the case in other countries where there are many dialects and languages, such as in Europe.

3. Keep the voice mail message very short.

4. People do not have the patience for a long message.

5. If you are bilingual use a separate phone number for your second language contacts. (It goes back to people's patience.) Two-language voice mail messages, on one number, is twice the wait for your contact to leave a message.

6. Speak clearly, and keep the message moving quickly.

7. Do not do advertising with your personal voice mail message.

8. I prefer not to mention my business name in my voice mail message.

9. Some of you are not going to like this next suggestion. I believe in spreading the Christian word, however, not in your voice mail. We are doing business to help people with their real estate. Our example of our Christian beliefs will be revealed in the manner in which we conduct our business and personal affairs with others.

I'M GLAD YOU ASKED

Many people have gotten their worst cheatings from people who started their business relationships talking about what wonderful Christians they are. I observe from their actions, not what they tell me. I wish for God to Bless all of you. Not on your voice mail.

This is the message I leave:

1. Hello, this is Bret Ehlers and it is a terrific day.
2. Please speak slowly and clearly.
3. Leave your first and last name and the telephone number where you would like me to reach you.
4. In fact leave your phone number twice with area code.
5. I will respond as quickly as possible.
6. Have a great day!

This will allow people to quickly leave you a message and not be aggravated with a long message wait time.

To Your Success

It is a terrific day!

Coach Bret Ehlers

I was told that Fanny Mae or the regulations that we have a limit as to how many mortgages you can have at any given time. Something in the ball park of 9 of them. With that said, is there a difference in the limit of the amount of properties that you can refinance like out from a hard money loan? Or is that considered to be the same? We look forward to your responses.

I would love to see you max out the Fannie Mae lending requirement. By the way, 10 is the maximum with your personal residence.

If you want some great evening reading, here is a link to all of the information on their lending limits and requirements.

https://www.fanniemae.com/content/guide/selling/b2/2/03.html

As for hard money loans, there are no limits except as designated by the funding source. Hard money is private funding and not guaranteed by the tax payer.

Hard money is generally too expensive for long term, fixed loans. You will want to look for other sources for long term loan structuring such as private or conventional loans.

To Your Success

It is a terrific day!

Coach Bret Ehlers

I have a question. When securing a deal through a FSBO, can the owner unknowingly use the property as collateral for other loans they may be trying to get or is there some sort of code that pops up to inform all creditors that we have an arrangement? I look forward to some informative chat. Aloha.

Every investor should secure their position on title with all For Sale by Owner (FSBO) agreements. Some investors want to conduct a "Table Top" closing with the FSBO and file the documents themselves to save a little money in the transaction. This is not encouraged.

FSBO real estate closings should be treated in the same manner as a closing where there is funding from a financial institution or alternative funding source, such as private or hard money. Work with your Title Company or Closing Attorney to search title, verify current title insurance, and file the appropriate documents on title at the County Recorder's Office to protect your transaction position.

The title search is to know other commitments the FSBO may have on the property. Are the bank payments current? Are all property taxes paid to date and is the property clear of mechanic liens and judgments? Many times the seller will fail to inform you of additional obligations they have where the property is commitment for collateral.

In some cases, you may want, or need to keep the transaction private from prying public eyes. Your Title Company or Closing Attorney can achieve this by recording a "Notice of Interest". A recorded Land Trust can provide the ultimate title protection in a FSBO transaction.

Be sure to conduct the following steps:

1. Title Search.

2. Current active Title Insurance. Paying to update the title insurance is not needed until you sell the property to the new owner occupant.
3. Freeze all Home Equity Lines of Credit (HELOC). You will not want the owner to continue borrowing money against the HELOC after you take possession of the property.
4. Record your interest on title.

When you follow these steps, even if the owner "broke contract" and used the property for collateral in another transaction you would be in a protected position on title ahead of all future events.

To Your Success

It is a terrific day!

Coach Bret Ehlers

Aloha. As we continue to research FSBO owner properties, I see many of them with the description of the title saying that it is a "Quiet Title". Are these red flags or a cause for concern? As I research some definitions it seems to involve some legal filing and litigation. Could someone please chime in and educate us? Thanks so much and we look forward to hearing from you.

A Quiet Title Action is a lawsuit to establish ownership of real property and cleanse the title to preclude any future claim by others to the title of the property.

This is done by an attorney who specializes in this aspect of law and will cost you up to $5,000 for the legal work. Every State's laws are different.

Typically, this will become an issue with certain circumstances involving the death of the property owner.

The purpose of the quiet title action is to validate the legal ownership of the title, eliminate all previous lien claims, and once again make the title marketable and able to obtain title insurance.

To Your Success

It is a terrific day!

Coach Bret Ehlers

I am wanting to understand the process of transitioning from a owner financed deal into a refinanced deal into a conventional mortgage. What are some of the steps involved with this?

Refinancing a seller financed transaction is one of the easiest actions you will do, Les.

From the beginning of the transaction, have your mortgage broker work with the buyer who is committed on the seller financed contract. The mortgage broker will do the work to get the property refinanced with the subject buyer. Close at the Title Company where you will receive your paycheck.

Use the skills of your team members to do what they do well so that you keep doing what makes you the money: Finding properties to match to buyers.

To Your Success

It is a terrific day!

Coach Bret Ehlers

We are looking at purchasing a multi-unit property. There are 10 units spread over 3 buildings. The units are presently divided into condos (10 separate parcels). If we are the successful bidders, we would consider having those combined back into one parcel. We intend to buy, fix, and hold the property for cash flow purposes. We would own the buildings and the land.

Is there a different tax treatment (depreciation, etc.) or other consideration for condos v. apartments that may inform our decision whether to combine or leave separate the units in each building?

I would definitely leave the existing title separation intact for each unit. To separate each unit was expensive for any zoning changes, engineering and titling.

This will also give you greater versatility in exit strategies and property uses.

This is a huge bonus to you.

As for the tax ramifications you will want to speak with your tax professional for your personal situation.

Don't forget to mention to your tax professional about having them do a Cost Segregation to depreciate the project in 7 to 15 years instead of the standard 39 ½ years.

To Your Success

It is a terrific day!

Coach Bret Ehlers

ACKNOWLEDGEMENTS

IN MEMORY OF DUSTY (FRED) TINGLEY 03-15-1950 to 07-31-2011

17 years ago Dusty Tingly introduced me to Cris and Jeff, two young entrepreneurs who were providing experienced help to new real estate investors to keep the new investor out of transaction trouble.

Because of the leadership and extreme determination of Cris, Jeff, and their later business partner Jim, I have witnessed their early beginnings become a superior model and standard of excellence untouched in the real estate training industry. I am honored to be part of their organization.

In the early years of my real estate business I wish I had known you could hire experienced real estate professionals to keep you out of trouble. If I had just known about Lease Options I would not have lost money on my first transaction.

I now have the privilege of being surrounded by a new group of incredible individuals. We have obtained the highest student success in the industry through student accountability.

Greg McCluskey - Our fearless leader who has an uncanny insight for individuals and process evaluation to implement successful operating systems.

Mark Sanderson - The master Corporate Ninja. He knows and sees all. A Special Thanks to Mark for the inspiration to develop this book and the push for me to complete it.

Carter Brown - aka The Black Panther. We all want to be as calculated and efficient as Carter.

Tim Bell - Makes learning the business fun while he kicks your butt.

Randy Cochrane - Always the calm in the storm. The master technology multi-tasker.

Kristiin Sabey - Dusty's third team member. She is the ultimate example of unselfishly loving and caring for the students while giving them a gentle nudge.

John Benson - Never a complaint and always a happy greeting with a smile though he deals with life and death health issues daily.

Erin Spainhower - The real captain of the ship without the stripes.

Taylor Ballstaedt - The sparkle and sunshine on the team.

Jack Ehlers - My Father took me with him from 5 years old. He taught me the architectural and construction business, the value of hard work and the importance of being self-employed if you want to have the ultimate financial life.

Bill Card - My Father's best friend who taught me massive wealth is found in finding solutions to problems. "You better pray for a lot of problems if you want to be really wealthy."

Ron Brunner - A great example of "You can have success in business and be a nice guy too."

Steve Welch - A driven mentor who gave me the tough love and success lessons I needed in my days of despair and doubt. Because of Heidi and Steve I have been able to make success happen again.

Bill Gatten - My good friend and mentor who taught me how to correctly and safely buy all real estate with no money.

Paul Halliday - My close friend, gym buddy, Rotarian and business attorney. When I was destitute, deep in legal battles and could not pay him, Paul stayed by my side to the bitter end. His friendship, unwavering help and faith in me would help me to return to my former wealth despite the tumultuous storms.

Dr. David Sessions - My sincerest appreciation to my close friend who has cared for me and nursed me back to health. Dave has helped to keep me functioning physically and mentally from a severe construction accident 18 years ago, which I should never have survived.

Heaven doesn't want me yet. Hell is afraid I will take over. I know I still have more people to help and more lives to change.

Eric Laver - My multi-millionaire best friend and long time next door neighbor who in the beginning, pushed me beyond my comfort level and perceived limitations. I am grateful to him for his tough love and persistence through my personal growth process in my pursuit of success. Growth is painful at all levels.

My sincerest thanks and appreciation to these wonderful people in my life.

No one achieves great accomplishments all on their own. I love and care for all of you.

Made in the USA
San Bernardino, CA
09 April 2016